D1515715

Lie Machines

Lie Machines

How to Save Democracy from Troll Armies,
Deceitful Robots, Junk News Operations, and
Political Operatives

PHILIP N. HOWARD

Yale UNIVERSITY PRESS

New Haven and London

Yale University Press books may be purchased in quantity for
educational, business, or promotional use. For information, please
e-mail sales.press@yale.edu (US office) or sales@yaleup.co.uk
(UK office).

Set in Minion type by Integrated Publishing Solutions, Grand
Rapids, Michigan.
Printed in the United States of America.

Library of Congress Control Number: 2019953622
ISBN 978-0-300-25020-6 (hardcover : alk. paper)

A catalogue record for this book is available from the British
Library.

This paper meets the requirements of ANSI/NISO Z39.48-1992
(Permanence of Paper).

10 9 8 7 6 5 4 3 2 1

For Elaine Howard, Mom,
who raised me to help battle lie machines

Contents

Preface

In the summer of 2019, President Donald J. Trump held a social media summit at the White House. The guests, however, were not representatives from the firms that own social media platforms. Instead, they were extremist, ultraconservative conspiracy theorists. The president nevertheless praised them for their work, calling them real journalists, vital opinion leaders, and assets to democracy. Let's be clear, though: the White House had brought together some of the producers, distributors, and marketers of big political lies. The summit attendees had a long record of disseminating racism, sexism, purposeful disinformation, and subtle misinformation over social media. The president validated and celebrated their work, and by inviting them to the White House, he elevated the purveyors of big political lies to the status of a central feature of modern democracy.

But this event was not just about celebrating the role of misinformation in public life. It was actually a form of campaign coordination. In preparing for the next big presidential campaign, the sitting president of the United States was rewarding his extended team with praise and validation, bringing them into the center of political power. He was acknowledging their role in his own political career, setting expectations for the campaign ahead, and sending clear signals on how he thought political news and information should be created.

I wish this book weren't necessary. In *New Media Campaigns and the Managed Citizen,* I analyzed how political actors used the internet to manipulate voters in the United States. In *The Digital Origins of Dictatorship and Democracy,* I described how new information technologies were helping democracy advocates dismantle the tough structures of authoritarianism. In *Pax Technica,* I wrote about how behavioral data from networked devices was increasingly being used to make political inferences—sometimes for the collective good and sometimes for social control. This current book is about the teams of people, such as those invited to the White House and others encircling some of the world's most prominent public figures, who do the work of embedding new information technologies into our political lives but use those technical systems to misinform us, distract us, and discourage sensible deliberation.

What connects these arguments is that, first and foremost, politics is a sociotechnical system constituted by both ideology and technology. Any framework for understanding politics that is simply about elections, political parties, and government, or that assigns technology a minor role in explaining current affairs, won't produce compelling explanations for political outcomes. Second, any sensible definition of democracy—or authoritarianism—must include elements of its information infrastructure. In an important way, this is because the features of a democracy may be abstract or found in broad generalizations and vague organizational arrangements that are rarely exercised or surprisingly fragile. But information policy, infrastructure standards, and cultures of technology use are the clear, specific, regular examples of democracy in action and practice. Social media platforms in particular provide the structure for our political lives, they regularize our civic engagement, and they offer the most comprehensive evidence of whether we are living in a democracy or a dictatorship.

If ruling elites, lobbyists, and shady politicians can use new information technology for political redlining or creating astroturf movements, they will. As you'll see in the chapters ahead, political redlining is the process of restricting our supply of political information based on assumptions about our demographics and our present or past opinions. It occurs when political consultants delimit which population is less likely to vote and then ignore that population, spending time serving only likely voters. Sometimes campaign managers dedicate resources to ensuring that a certain group won't vote.

I'm hopeful, positivist, and unbending in this book in that I have an expansive and inclusive definition of what I mean by "big political lies" and I have faith that exposing and correcting them with evidence can improve policy making, governance, and public life.

There are so many variations of political lies that I will not philosophize about their nuances. Yet I do believe that evidence and truth can disabuse us of bad ideas based on misinformation, disinformation, untruth, half-truth, distortion, or omission of facts. If pressed to offer a formal definition of a *lie machine,* I would say that this book is about the social and technical mechanisms for putting an untrue claim into service of political ideology. It's not PR, and it's more than political campaign messaging. And *computational propaganda* is the use of algorithms to produce, distribute, and market untruths that serve ideology. Some writers prefer *disinformation, misinformation, propaganda,* or other terms for these fibs. For me, however, understanding the nuanced distinctions among types of political lies is not as important as understanding the political economy and technological basis of their creation and success. So in the pages that follow, I am not rigid in using just one term, and I use the term most sensibly descriptive for the example at hand. In my mind, the examples in this book are all in the family of big political lies.

Authoritarian governments will look, almost by definition, for ways to use new information technologies for social control. Their strategy involves seeding multiple conflicting stories about events and using technologies to prevent the public from having sensible debates about those events. Democracy advocates will always look for creative ways to catch dictators off guard using information technology. What I didn't expect, before I began research in this field, is that authoritarian regimes would use such techniques on voters in democracies. And then I didn't expect politicians, lobbyists, and political parties in democracies to adapt those techniques for use on their own citizens. I assumed that electoral administrators, public officials, and courts would prevent the political communication techniques of dictatorships from diffusing into democracies.

People—and Their Technology—Make Politics

In 2014, I wrote an opinion piece suggesting that bot use was on the rise and that politicians should pledge not to use them on voters. "Would political campaign managers in a democracy like the United States use bots?" I asked. I concluded, "The question is not whether political parties in democracies will start using bots on one another—and us—but when."

I don't believe that politicians or political campaign managers in democracies read that piece. In 2015, I wrote *Pax Technica,* a book about the shifting location of political power from the organizations of government to the technology firms of

Silicon Valley. Much of the evidence in the book was from authoritarian regimes and failed states where technology platforms were providing governance goods that public agencies
couldn't provide. These were also countries where political elites
were using information technology as a tool for social control.

This book continues my argument that politics is best
understood as a sociotechnical system. There is a global economy of political lies, and in these pages I explain how that
economy has evolved because of how we use our technology
to organize data and how technology innovation uses our
data. The biggest political lies are the result of complex interactions between people and our technologies, and any sensible
causal explanation for modern politics must dig into that com-
plexity. To tell this story you must have a global perspective,
and you must feature people and technology as key actors. The
causal story is a global one because the production, distribution, and marketing of political lies involve people and places
all over the world, even if the targets for misinformation are
the citizens of one country. The causes of democratic malaise,
rising populism, poor political decision making, and declining
voter sophistication are complex and conjoined: people produce and consume the lies, but the algorithms, data sets, and
information infrastructure determine the impact of those lies.

What Is a Political Lie?

I have an expansive definition of what makes a *political lie*.
Several key aspects of political lies are covered in chapter 1. But
there are so many variations of misleading political content
that I don't believe the nuances are more important than the
consequences of their production, distribution, and marketing to citizens. Looking across the examples used in this book,

there are incorrect opinions and clear untruths. There is misinformation and disinformation, deliberately crafted to be so extremist, sensationalist, and conspiratorial that they effectively become lies. The common ingredients include incendiary and polarizing commentary and points of fact that are so wrong that the main outcome of accepting or tolerating the inaccuracies is an incendiary, polarizing conclusion. Content that promotes undue skepticism, negative emotions, and contrarian views for the sake of "teaching the controversy" or text and video messages that bring anxiety or aversion to dialogue and new evidence also fall into the broad category of political lies.

Writing about all the torrid details of political lies, manipulations, and deception may seem a soul-crushing task. But I think that these lie machines have caused several of our democratic organizations and institutions to grind to a halt. Some elections and referenda generate incredible outcomes which are almost mistakes in that such large numbers of voters had such poor-quality information that their deliberations resulted in solvable errors.

Many people believe things that are demonstrably false. Telling organized lies helps some politicians win and stay in office, where they use bad information to make poor decisions. They generate new conspiracies and deepen public distrust, and then voters go back to the polls on election day equipped with even more grievances and less information. We can't save our democracies unless we understand these mechanisms.

People in several countries are now governed by political leaders who have rejected, not just specific scientific advice, but the overall notion that carefully collected evidence is the best way to understand the world. Such deliberate use of lie machines is deeply distressing. But we are threatened with more than emotional distress. Purposefully organized ignorance may end up destroying our ability to deliberate sensibly.

Innovative Falsehoods

Many people wonder what's new about the political lies and manipulations we've experienced in recent years. Certainly, the history of propaganda and political rumor mongering is long. The first broadsheets, newspapers, and, later, newswires were regularly accused of spreading made-up stories serving various political agendas. But compared to today, such print journalism was harder to produce, distribute, and market to vast numbers of people.

The complex political misinformation efforts of yesteryear took significant physical resources to orchestrate. For example, after World War II, the East German Stasi faked Nazi era records and deposited them at the bottom of Černé Jezero Lake in what was then Czechoslovakia. In 1964, the records were then "found" and shared at a dramatic press conference, thereby ending the careers of some West German politicians and impeding the prosecution of war criminals. Operation Neptune, as it was dubbed, was later revealed to be one of the Stasi's most complex disinformation campaigns. In another example, in 1974 Greek Cypriots were accused of burning a Turkish mosque on the island nation. This news was broadcast all over Turkey, giving the Turkish president a ratings boost and national support for invading Cyprus. A Turkish general later admitted that Turkish troops burned the mosque to foment dispute. There certainly is a long history to fake news production, but in the past, it was mostly employed in times of war and crisis and was produced by major governments.

Things changed significantly with the creation of the internet, which quickly became a tool for automating political lies. The first known use of a political bot is UseNet's Serdar Argic account in the late 1980s. This early bot searched for the

term "Turkey" and then posted denials of the Armenian Genocide. Like some of the latest political bots, its reach was somewhat accidental because this simple keyword trigger meant
that this political misinformation was posted in lists dedicated
to cooking and Christmas and Thanksgiving celebrations. But
most such early examples share similar features: there were
some elements of truth to the storylines, and significant financial and personnel resources were dedicated to executing the
plan for disseminating the lies. They were large, one-off projects that couldn't be easily repeated and refined over time.

What makes today's lie machines different is their low
cost of production, the great speed of dissemination over social media, and the expanding industry of marketing agencies
to help place and amplify computational propaganda. In 2014,
the Columbian Chemicals Plant explosion hoax scared US
voters with the story of a factory in Louisiana that had been
attacked by ISIS (the Islamic State in Iraq and Syria). All the
content was faked: images were doctored to appear to have
come from CNN, falsified pages were placed on Wikipedia, and
fake user accounts on multiple platforms spread the junk news.
Many more examples of such lie machines are covered in the
pages ahead—examples of campaigns that ran for months, taking advantage of the affordances of social media advertising
technologies. For now, let's just state that what makes modern
lie machines special is that they are much less expensive to
run, are based on quantitative models about information circulation, and allow constant experimentation and testing to
perfect, refine, and reproduce messaging. They are produced at
an industrial scale. This has made them a pernicious threat to
public life.

Along with some big data analysis, this book makes use
of interviews of people who are involved in the creation of lie

machines. As is the norm in contemporary ethnography, in-
terviewees were offered pseudonyms and some observations
and experiences have been compiled and combined to create
archetypes of individuals working in the production, distribution, and marketing of political lies. Company names have
been changed. While I worked with many of the interview
subjects, as a security measure, the files linking real people and
real companies with their pseudonyms were not shared across
country research teams or centralized. For example, fieldwork
with firms in Poland and Brazil involved interviewing staff
and experts, visiting several workplaces, and tracking their
activities. But in this book I have aggregated observations and
created corporate pseudonyms using the word equivalent to
imitation in Polish and Brazilian Portuguese. Because these
firms create fake social media profiles that emulate real citizens, I call the Polish company Imitacja Consulting and the
Brazilian company Imitação Services.

Lie machines are a global problem, with a treadmill of
production, distribution, and marketing that crosses international borders. Political actors are getting very good at producing big lies, social media algorithms provide an effective
way of distributing those lies, and the science of marketing lies
to the right audience is improving. I believe that such successful marketing actually cultivates the audience—even makes
the audience grow—resulting in sustained support for the dictators, lobbyists, and dishonest politicians who are good at
building and maintaining lie machines.

I hope that understanding how lie machines work can
help us take them apart. The big lie machines are a mix of
human and technical practices. Understanding this gives us a
wider surface for intervention, with both social and technical
solutions. Treating the problem this way makes it easier to

craft legislation and regulation for particular industries, hold social media firms to account, identify practices that should be criminalized, and seek technical fixes to the challenges besieging democracy.

1

The Science and Technology
of Lie Machines

How is it possible to make convincing arguments, without evidence, about the causes of or solutions to important social problems? Lie machines do this work, and they seem to be more and more active in public life. These social and technical systems generate and spread political lies by subverting the people, organizations, and institutions in which we have most confidence. We tend to trust our instincts for evaluating the truth, and we tend to trust friends and family as sources of good information; as sources of news, many of us prefer social media to professional print media.[1]

Lie machines vary in size and scope. Some are large and permanent, others more liminal—temporary teams formed for a campaign or an election. But the inventory is growing, and in authoritarian regimes lie machines are often partnered with overt political surveillance initiatives. China employs two million people to write 448 million messages a year.[2] The previous Mexican president had seventy-five thousand highly automated accounts cheering for him and his policies.[3] Vietnam has trained ten thousand students to deploy as cyber troops to combat online dissent.[4] The Thai government runs a special program rewarding children who report on any neighbors and family who protest using social media.[5] Huge bursts of automated activity occur whenever the presidents of the Philippines or Turkey score political victories.

Unfortunately, these massive mechanisms for social control don't only operate in authoritarian countries. In democracies, the surveillance is done by the social media firms themselves and not directly turned over to the government. However, the data gleaned by surveilling social media activity is still packaged and analyzed—it's just that the customers for this information are politicians, lobbyists, political consultants, and advertisers who are interested in what we're thinking about. Since 2016, every major democracy has suffered in some way: policy conversations go off the rails because of fake news; public understanding of critical issues is warped by well-advertised misinformation; surprising domestic political outcomes are shaped by hostile foreign actors.

Lie machines are large, complex mechanisms made up of people, organizations, and social media algorithms that generate theories to fit a few facts, while leaving you with a crazy conclusion easily undermined by accurate information. By manipulating data and algorithms in the service of a political agenda, the best lie machines generate false explanations that seem to fit the facts.

Lie machines have three main components, and if we examine the parts and understand how they work together, we can devise ways to take them apart or even prevent them from being built. The first component is the producer of lies that serve an ideology or the interests of political elites. These producers are often political candidates, campaign teams, political parties, and agencies of authoritarian governments, but they can be marginal political actors who just want to disrupt public life. The second component is the distributor of lies: the algorithm that social media firms provide for spreading content. Social networks like Facebook, Instagram, Twitter, and WhatsApp—and the data they collect about our political preferences—are the distribution system for political lies. The third key component is the marketer of political lies, usually a consulting firm, lobbyist, or political hired gun who profit from selling, amplifying, and promoting disinformation. Big lie machines have production, distribution, and marketing systems that cross international borders, and in the chapters ahead we'll examine each component and evaluate how it works.

Large data sets have revolutionized politics by making it easier for politicians to understand what voters want. For decades politicians have used polling data and surveys to interpret what voters are thinking about. But traditional polling methods have always had limitations. And the polling data they gathered was either attitudinal (what people think) or aspirational (what people hope for). Now we have behavioral data about what people *actually do,* so lobbyists, campaign managers, and politicians can make much more powerful inferences about voters: Do you say you are pro-life on abortion issues but use your personal credit cards to buy contraceptives? What kinds of magazines do you subscribe to, and which online news sources do you spend the most time reading? How might your shopping choices reveal something about your thinking on environmental issues? All this data yields political information.

Lobbyists, political campaign managers, and politicians use social media to communicate directly with voters. Tools like Twitter and Facebook allow campaigners to communicate without worrying about how journalists and editors may change or interpret the campaign messages. And increasingly, campaign managers employ automated tools to do this, with data generated by technology users—by us. Such automation allows a campaign to plan its communications far in advance, so that a greater volume of personalized, prefigured content can be sent to each voter even more quickly. Sometimes we are aware of the data trail we leave behind, but rarely can we see how it gets aggregated and merged with other data sets. And seldom do we see how it is made relational—put in context with data from our neighbors, friends, and families.

It can be hard to fully grasp where all that data comes from. Even though we are aware that our smartphones and computers keep track of our activities, we rarely think of the smart refrigerators, cars, lightbulbs, and other everyday objects that increasingly track our behaviors. And seldom do we see how this data is applied or passed to sophisticated artificial intelligence for analysis. Globally, each day, we generate five hundred million tweets, send 294 billion emails, put four petabytes of content on Facebook, send sixty-five billion messages on WhatsApp, and do five billion searches on Google. That's a lot of data about our thoughts, feelings, and activities. Yet there is even more data that connected devices around us collect—details that can also reveal much about our behavior. For example, every day each connected car generates four terabytes of data about how the engine is performing and where it is taking the driver.[6] Our cellphones and portable electronics generate similar data about performance, contents, and where we take them.

The Great Transformation

The internet has always been a powerful tool for political communication. But the tone and timbre of what was communicated, and for which purposes, has changed over time. In the early days of the internet, when lobbyists wanted to push a piece of legislation or candidates ran for election, they could use the web to publish their platform, buy online banner ads, and trade messages with voters and supporters. This was still a one-to-many mode of communication, in that the political campaign would put content online and anyone could visit the webpage or consume the content if they were interested. More recently, social media platforms have introduced new mechanisms for political communication, including ways for users to involve their own networks of family and friends in clusters of political affiliation, content sharing, and data mining.

The people who follow your social media accounts are interested in what you say, and social media firms sell access to your entire network of family and friends. More importantly, social media platforms allow your followers to pass content to their own networks of family and friends. Campaign communications conducted over the internet can involve generic messages. But many messages that arrive on social media often look like personal communication because, by definition, we've included our friends and family in our social networks.

Political campaign managers have quickly made use of the networks of trust and reciprocity we reveal to social media firms. And many kinds of campaigners have taken advantage of network effects to spread appeals for support. During the 2008 US presidential election, Barack Obama's campaign organization used social media networks with great success. The campaign's technology strategy allowed supporters to network among themselves, offloading the organizational costs of campaigning onto energetic volunteers.[7] And during the Arab Spring protests of 2010–12, democracy advocates used social media networks to support one-to-one communication on a large scale to coordinate massive protests that brought down authoritarian regimes in Tunisia, Egypt, Libya, and Yemen.[8] Regimes that didn't collapse were forced to make a range of political and financial concessions to appease popular demands. Having seen activists use social media as a mechanism for social mobilization, powerful lobbyists and authoritarian regimes began using the very same technologies for social control and to advance their causes.[9]

Microtargeting is the process of preparing and delivering customized messages to voters or consumers. Television, newspaper, and radio advertising can be targeted at broad categories of people. For example, men generally respond well to certain colors, keywords, pictures, and narratives, while women respond to others. Political campaign messages can be scripted to contain cultural cues that might attract or be familiar to, for example, urbanites, retirees, college students, or pregnant women. Campaign ads can be targeted using several demographic categories at once. As a concept, microtargeting involves preparing and delivering a message that is customized for particular individuals. With the right data, microtargeting can even design—in real time—ads customized to certain individuals. By assembling data from our personal credit card records, the national census, and our social media use, political campaigns can make some good guesses about our opinions on the issues of the day.

Some of the most effective lie machines, however, are built by political parties, authoritarian regimes, and radical social movements. Organized parties and movements attract supporters by using as much personal data on people as possible, whether targeting constituents, voters, members, consumers, or any other group of people. Sometimes this data is used for what I elsewhere term *political redlining*.[10] This is the process of deciding which people your campaign *doesn't* need to engage with. If, for example, people of color under a certain income level rarely vote, or if they always vote for your opponent, it may not be worth spending time in their neighborhood trying to convince them to vote for you. If a city has consistently voted for one party for decades and there's no evidence that public sentiment is changing, why put campaign resources into advertising there? Of course, this is a rhetorical question, because it *is* healthy for civic life to have consistent, high-quality information and debate running in every neighborhood.

Bad Prospects

For the most part, when authoritarian governments, industry lobbyists, and shady politicians get hold of personal data, it is because they want to figure out how to build an effective campaign for winning support and legitimacy. Sometimes such data helps a politician or lobbyist better understand voters. When a crisis emerges or a major decision is needed, this data can allow political leaders to take the pulse of the community they serve. But usually personal data isn't used for substantive engagement; instead, it is applied for strategic reasons, to mobilize supporters and deepen existing commitments. Social media platforms are the delivery mechanism for the misinformation, for maneuvering or manipulating the individuals in the data set. In the chapters ahead, we'll see how many kinds of strategies, purposes, and outcomes there can be.

Most citizens don't know how much information about them is being used: it is bought and sold by campaigns, advertising firms, political consultants, and social media platforms. Sometimes political campaigns have clear sponsors and declare their interests, but at other times such motives are hidden. Sometimes the public can trace who is spending what resources on which ads during a campaign season, but at other times the advertising is discrete and directed and not archived anywhere. Most democracies have independent elections regulators tasked with ensuring fair play, but not all such agencies are well funded. Sometimes campaigns deliberately spread misinformation, lies, and rumors about rivals and opponents that poison public life.

As far as I have observed over several years of investigation, political campaigns in the United States—and many other democracies—rarely give much thought to managing the data they collect. They don't have data management plans the way hospitals, government agencies, or even private firms do. Usually individual campaign managers and consultants maintain their own data sets, and this data travels with them from campaign to campaign. Political campaigns that are well resourced may commission surveys and political polls, and sometimes the polling firm will provide copies of the raw data, but usually the pollster writes up summary reports and interprets the trends for the campaign. Political campaigns that are very well resourced will hire consultants to build and maintain specialized political data sets that merge data from many sources: campaign contact records about voters, party membership information, public records, survey results, census data, social media data, and credit card data. Usually the consultants treat this information as their intellectual property and the political client doesn't have access to the raw data. Some consulting firms build trusted relationships with a political party so that strategic information that the party contributes stays among groups that share a political agenda.

Political campaigns have few systematic safeguards to protect data. As the 2016 Russian hack of the US Democratic Party, or the 2019 Russian hack of the UK Conservative Party illustrates, even the wealthiest political parties have trouble keeping personal records secure. Some countries have privacy commissioners, but only since the Facebook–Cambridge Analytica scandal—in which millions of Facebook users' personal profiles were data mined and used for creating political ads— have countries started looking deeply into campaign practices around data. Most organizations and websites, such as social media platforms, credit card companies, and campaigns, have terms of service agreements. But usually these make a weak commitment to keeping data safe, saying that they will share data only with third parties they have evaluated for trustworthiness. In my experience, when you look at the list of third parties, you'll see quite a long list of subcontractors, individual consultants, and small ad agencies with their own inadequate data management practices.

If you want to explore what kind of political inferences can be made from the data you have been generating over the years, simply review your credit card records or get a copy of your credit history. First, know that this collection of data is only a fraction of what exists about you. It is sometimes called core data because along with demographics such as your age, gender, and race, it is a very basic set of facts about who you are, where you've been, and what you've been doing. It probably contains straightforward information about your address— probably all the addresses you've ever had—and that information is used for direct mailing campaigns. But core data usually also includes telephone number records so consultants can make robocalls or have third-party call centers contact you. Depending on the country you live in, there may be publicly available records of the political donations you have made or the political parties you belong to. When information about your political affiliations is married to your credit card records, a campaign professional has the data to make a whole lot of inferences about how to organize the facts into a theory you are likely to believe.

Democracy Encoded

New technologies always inspire hot debate about the nature of politics and public life. When activists used Facebook to organize protests across North Africa, journalist Malcolm Gladwell argued that only face-to-face interaction could make a true social movement and a real revolution.[11] Technology writer Clay Shirky countered that it no longer made sense to distinguish street politics from internet politics.[12] Evgeny Morozov of the *New Republic* agreed that the internet was useful in politics, but mostly for dictators, internet activist Eli Pariser argued that too many of us were using technology to immerse ourselves in information bubbles that protect us from exposure to challenging new ideas.[13] I argued that everyone was focusing on the wrong internet—that we should be concerned about data from our own devices shaping politics, not content from our browsers.[14] This was the means by which political elites would "manage citizens" in the years ahead.[15]

Unsurprisingly, research has disproved some of these claims and confirmed others. Gladwell was wrong in that social media proved to be a sufficient cause of several contemporary political uprisings and revolutions.[16] Shirky was prescient in identifying the ways in which the internet supported new modes of organizing, modes that could catch dictators off guard.[17] Morozov was correct in suspecting that the bad guys would quickly learn to use new technologies in their organizational efforts and would work to catch democracy advocates and put them in jail, though his fatalism muddled his thinking. But as we'll see in the chapters ahead, it turns out that the big, modern mechanisms for political manipulation depend on both our social media output and device-level data about our behavior: algorithms use such data to render the best models for doing targeted political advertising and organizing voter contact.

Despite all the debate about the impact of the internet on politics and public life over the past decade, no one thought that social media could be used to threaten so deeply the primary exercises of democracy: elections and referenda. Spreading vast quantities of political misinformation before voting day, in cleverly targeted ways, was not what social media was built for. Social media platforms were created from the ground up for advertising, but not to sell us political candidates. Yet as these platforms sought ways to monetize their assets—peoples' attention—they purposefully took advantage of our cognitive biases. More specifically, social media platforms served up our cognitive biases to political and ideological projects. At first, it was the toughest strongmen in Egypt, Turkey, and Pakistan who used social media as an instrument for social control. In democracies, far-right and far-left parties occasionally pushed the envelope with campaign tricks that either broke the law or violated the spirit of democratic discourse. What we didn't anticipate was the degree to which mainstream politicians in established democracies would use social media to manipulate their own publics.

In 2016, the campaign to have UK voters reject the European Union generated unusually bold lies about the costs and benefits of being an EU member. This campaign effectively used social media to poison debate and muddy issues. In the United States, pro-Trump bots, trolls, and ad buys greatly inflated a range of sensational, conspiracy, and extremist myths about Hillary Clinton. The Russian government and domestic groups sharing political affinities sank significant resources into the distribution of polarizing content over Facebook and Twitter, expanding to include other social media platforms such as Instagram and YouTube in the years after the election of Donald Trump. Globally, many democratic elections since 2016 have suffered from some loss of credibility because of the operation of similar lie machines. In countries such as Brazil and the Philippines, populist leaders have embraced the same social media strategies used by authoritarian governments. Even in strong democracies like Canada and Germany, a few shady politicians get caught using these tools to suppress voter turnout, misinform voters, and undermine public confidence in electoral outcomes.

My research team at the University of Oxford has misinformation trends on social media in dozens of countries. During the presidential election of 2016 in the United States, there was a one-to-one ratio of junk news to professional news shared by voters over Twitter. In other words, for each link to a story produced by a professional news organization, there was another link to content that was extremist, sensationalist, or conspiratorial or to other forms of junk news. This is the highest level of junk news circulation in any of the countries we have studied.[18] Critically for politics in the United States, this misinformation was concentrated in the most competitive districts—where small shifts in popular opinion had big consequences.[19] Moreover, the audience for misinformation was primarily Republican voters who supported Trump.[20] Misinformation campaigns are often launched using highly automated accounts and fake users, and such accounts promoted significant amounts of content from Russian news sources, links to unverified material on WikiLeaks, and other forms of junk news. We have found that it is not just bot accounts that spread junk news; at the right volume level, junk news can permeate deeply into networks of human users.[21]

Just a few months after the 2016 US elections, we demonstrated that disinformation about national security issues, including from Russian sources, was being targeted at US military personnel and veterans and their families.[22] During the president's State of the Union address, we learned that junk news is particularly appetizing for far-right white supremacists and President Trump's supporters (though not "small c" conservatives).[23] Some of this junk content originates in accounts managed by foreign governments.

Foreign intervention in politics, using social media, is ongoing, and it doesn't just involve the Russian government. As protests started rocking Hong Kong in 2019, Chinese government propagandists activated their social media networks to convince the world that the activists were violent radicals with no popular appeal. By 2020, seven countries were running misinformation campaigns targeting citizens in other countries: along with Russia and China, there were similar operations in India, Iran, Pakistan, Saudi Arabia, and Venezuela.[24] Whether built to target neighboring countries or domestic voters, these mechanisms do the same thing—they produce, disseminate, and market lies.

What Is a Lie Machine?

A *lie machine* is a system of people and technologies that distribute false messages in the service of a political agenda. The system involved can include many kinds of organizations, individuals, and relationships, from formal paid-employment relationships to those of volunteer associations and affinity groups who produce content and share it over networks of family and friends. The people producing this have either a political or a financial incentive to do so—they work for political parties or they are political consultants and lobbyists for industry groups. But the most important people in these networks are citizens who make the mistake of passing a piece of misinformation from a junk news source, fake user, or political shill to broader networks of real citizens and voters. Some of the people involved in the mechanism are programmers who set up vast networks of highly automated accounts. These citizens have a disproportionate share of the public conversation because of the fake user accounts they control.

Social media platforms, search engines, and myriad devices provide the technology and infrastructure for delivering misinformation directly to citizens at key moments in a public conversation. Usually several technologies are used in a lie machine. For example, data from your credit card purchases may be used to create a digital political profile of you as a social media user. Then several of the platforms and websites you visit display political ads that are likely to trigger your interests and attention.

Whether through accidental sharing or purposeful distribution, an array of political actors and average citizens distribute and disseminate content by liking, retweeting, repurposing, and repackaging the content. Subtle alterations help the lies avoid spam filters, validity checks, and human editors and spread across social networks.

Unfortunately, there are many varieties of lies and what Caroline Jack calls "problematic information."[25] And the media's dependence on social media, analytics and metrics, sensationalism, novelty over newsworthiness, and clickbait gives the producers, distributors, and marketers of political lies the ability to project misinformation and disinformation to a wide audience.[26] *Misinformation* is contested information that reflects political disagreement and deviation from expert consensus, scientific knowledge, or lived experience. *Disinformation* is purposefully crafted and strategically placed information that deceives someone—tricks them—into believing a lie or taking action that serves someone else's political interests. *Junk news* is political news and information that is sensational, extremist, conspiratorial, severely biased, or commentary masked as news.

The messages, pictures, videos, and other content that lie machines distribute isn't simply false advertising. It can include very personal messages from platform users who are being paid by foreign governments to bait you to join an argument or spread a rumor. It can include highly customized posts about conspiracies. Paid advertising takes advantage of a platform's own means of generating a profit for itself, while direct messaging involves users who work for a political agenda.

The key distinction between misinformation and false advertising for commercial products is that the lies are in service of some political ideology. And generating social media content in the service of a party or an ideology increasingly takes a formal work arrangement, with teams under contract, storyboards and scripts, dedicated office space, and significant financial commitments. Sometimes individuals buy ads on their own or work as coordinated volunteers to drive a political figure off social media. But this work can also involve formal employment with agencies that coordinate large, agile teams that can be hired on short notice to support a political communication campaign.

Many kinds of political actors put technology in the service of power. In almost all countries, it is the far-right, ultra-conservative groups and populist leaders that get caught using such tools early and aggressively. Only on rare occasions have we caught left-wing populists and middle-of-the-road politicians putting these tools and techniques to work for a political agenda, and usually it's only after someone else has used a lie machine to attack them. Foreign governments meddle in the domestic affairs of neighboring countries, usually to sow local discord or target a politician whose ideas threaten the foreign government. When political parties do it, it's about projecting their values by stoking fear, uncertainty, and misunderstanding.

Lie machines are made up of parts—people and the technologies for disseminating the falsehoods they come up with. And when assembled properly, lie machines put information technology into service for a political ideology by generating computational propaganda. Deliberately using device networks, social media algorithms, and personal data to shape how we perceive the world is the work of regular advertisers but also of propagandists. Producing, distributing, and marketing propaganda is certainly an old craft, but these new, scaled-up mechanisms swiftly create and distribute content, with rapid testing and refinement, customized for individual consumption by that individual's personal and behavioral data.[27] This is not the broadcast era's propaganda of posters, government advertising, and leaflets dropped from airplanes. The modern lie machine is not a mass media instrument for broadcasting misleading information. It is a new, complex system of people and technologies with unique features.

The best lie machines involve components with three key functions: production, distribution, and marketing. The better these components work to promote a political lie, the greater the chances are of successfully manipulating public opinion on an issue. First, a well-running lie machine requires government agencies, political leaders, candidates for election, or political parties who produce misinformation in the service of their political agenda or big ideological project. Second, a lie machine needs a distribution system, which today takes the form of the platforms provided by social media firms. The distribution system of bots, fake accounts, and easily exploited social media algorithms provides a technical infrastructure for packaging the lie and delivering it to your inbox. The third important component of a lie machine is the marketing work and this usually involves consultants and commercial agencies who polish and bundle the information into junk news stories. They analyze both big-picture market trends and data about you to get the marketing strategy right. Political consultants, lobbyists, and advertisers make big money by refining such marketing strategies. In sum, the key components are the people who produce political lies, the social media firms that distribute the lies, and the consulting firms that market the lies to you.

Simply defined, *computational propaganda* is the misleading news and information that is created in the service of political interests and algorithmically distributed across social media networks. It can involve networks of highly automated Twitter accounts or fake users on Facebook. Sometimes the people running these campaigns simply pay for advertising and exploit the services that social media companies offer to all kinds of advertisers. Often the political campaigns or foreign governments that generate computational propaganda take advantage of the design of platforms. So for dating apps like Tinder, the automated accounts or fake users will flirt and then talk politics. For YouTube, the goal is to repackage mainstream content or create dedicated channels to keep users in a narrow stream of content. Strategies for Reddit involve creating crazy new conspiracy theories and encouraging users to transport those theories to other platforms. Doing so usually means breaking terms of service agreements, violating community norms, and using platform *affordances* in a way the engineers didn't intend. Occasionally it means breaking election law, privacy regulations, or consumer protection rules. But it happens anyway—sometimes because of inadequate enforcement of existing laws, regulations, and rules or inadequate public policy oversight. At times the firms themselves don't consistently enforce their own terms of service, because doing so would mean losing revenue or upsetting a group of users.

What Do Lie Machines Look Like?

Many people are questioning whether social media platforms are threatening democracy. Concentrated in just a few hands, these firms are aggregating large data sets about public and private life—including data on demographics and public attitudes and opinions. Making all this intelligence available for commercial use allows elite political actors to control the most valuable resource possible in a democracy: our attention. Information infrastructure is an invaluable asset to lobbyists seeking to pass legislation, foreign governments interested in controlling domestic conversations, and political campaign managers working to win an election.[28] While the internet has certainly opened new avenues for civic participation in political processes—inspiring hopes of a democratic reinvigoration— the parallel rise of big data analytics, black-box algorithms, and computational propaganda is raising significant concerns for policymakers worldwide. In many countries around the world, divisive social media campaigns have heightened ethnic tensions, revived nationalistic movements, intensified political conflict, and even resulted in political crises—while simultaneously weakening public trust in journalism, democratic institutions, and electoral outcomes.[29]

The first troll armies appeared in Russia in 2007, during Vladimir Putin's second term as president. I traveled there that summer to meet these early patriotic bloggers who went to camps on the outskirts of Moscow to talk about the future of their country—and learn to code. After multiple successful campaigns of misinformation, the use of trolls spread as other governments, political parties, and lobbyists saw Russia's troll armies in action. By 2016, some twenty-five countries were spending upward of $2.5 billion a year on large cohorts of commentators, reviewers, harassers, and advocates who manipulated public life over social media. By 2020, more than seventy countries had organized social media misinformation teams.

These days, troll armies take many different organizational shapes. In the Philippines, President Rodrigo Duterte paid a small army of social media users not just to post upbeat messages about his candidacy for president but to threaten and harass his critics and opponents. In a country with one of the highest rates of extrajudicial killing and journalist murder rates in the world, a few threatening social media messages can be enough to drive many reasonable people out of public life. Given the great variety of lie machines in operation, what is the best way to frame the problem, explain it, and work out the best ways to break the lie machines down?

Lie Machines as Sociotechnical Systems

For many years, being a social scientist has meant purposefully gathering large amounts of information about people, their relationships, and their ideas. But the internet has also affected how we do such research, because it has become harder and harder to build meaningful explanations of social phenomena without making room for the affordances of information infrastructure. We used to think that people were the primary causes of social change. Many disciplines of social science inquiry investigate the role of media, technology, and information infrastructure and treat these things as tools for individuals, networks, and communities. But increasingly we've had to admit that such a fundamental infrastructure as the internet both enables and limits our activities. Causal factors are often conjoined, and sensible explanations of modern politics need to give attention to the causal role of information technology.

A *sociotechnical system* is made up of people and their tools, and seeing both in interaction gives you a better analytical frame because you can observe how the material world provides both capacities for and constraints upon human action. We may all feel that we are agents, yet our ability to have an impact on the social and material world around us is largely determined by our access to information and our ability to communicate. Having a good education, consuming high-quality news, and using the latest information technology allows us to have an impact. These may give some of us the capacity to change the world, but for other people, not having access becomes a constraint.

Understanding the momentous changes and big challenges in how we do politics must mean understanding both people and technology. It is possible to be too technologically determinist, however. Arguing that the internet alone is responsible for social decay gets us nowhere. But it is also possible to be technologically underdetermined: we must also admit that the social media platforms we've built for ourselves have affordances that help us behave badly, circulate misinformation, cause other people harm, and degrade public life.

However, trying to understand computational propaganda only from a technical perspective—as hardware and algorithms—plays into the hands of those who use the technology to undermine democracy and the firms that profit when that happens.[30] The very act of describing something as purely technical or in very mechanistic terms may make it seem unbiased, inevitable, or easily fixed by an engineer or a change in settings. This is clearly a dangerous position to take, and we must look to the emerging discipline of social data science to help us understand the complex sociotechnical issues at play and the influence of technology on politics. As part of this process, social data science researchers must maintain a critical stance toward the data they use and analyze to ensure that they are critiquing as they go about describing, predicting, or recommending changes in the way technology and politics evolve. If academic research on computational propaganda does not engage fully with the systems of power and knowledge that produce it—the human actors and motivations behind it— then the very possibility of improving the role of social media platforms in public life evaporates.[31] We can only hope to understand and respond appropriately to a problem like computational propaganda by undertaking computational research alongside qualitative investigation. This lets us see and understand the sociotechnical system.

Computational propaganda, then, is both a social and a technical phenomenon. It is produced by an assembly of social media platforms, people, algorithms, and big data tasked with the manipulation of public opinion.[32] *Computational* propaganda is of course a recent form of the propaganda that has existed in our political systems for millennia—communications that deliberately subvert symbols, appealing to our baser emotions and prejudices and bypassing rational thought to achieve the specific goals of its promoters—and is understood as propaganda that is created or disseminated by computational means. Automation, scalability, and anonymity are hallmarks of computational propaganda. The pernicious advantage of computational propaganda is that it enables the rapid distribution of large amounts of content, sometimes personalized in order to fool users into thinking that messages originated in their extended network of family and friends. In this way, computational propaganda typically requires bots that automate content delivery, fake social media accounts that need little human curation, and junk news that is misinformation about politics and public life.[33]

Thus, the mechanism we need to understand—and rebuild—is one that involves both people and technology. People generate political misinformation; social media platforms such as Facebook, Instagram, and Twitter spread it around. Politicians generate negative messages; Twitter distributes the anger and outrage. Of course, journalists still generate high-quality journalism, and politicians do have positive, constructive ideas about public policy. But long-form, high-quality journalism and interesting new ideas about public policy aren't disseminated as widely as extremist, conspiratorial, and sensational junk news. If we analyze the entire mechanism, with its social and technical parts, can we redesign it to support democratic norms?

Taking the Lie Machines Apart

Public life is being torn apart. Lie machines sow distrust and infect political conversations with anger, moral outrage, and invective in ways that forestall consensus building. It is not simply that social media may have side effects, making us dependent on our screens for news and information, or that our mobile phones may be isolating us from our neighbors.[34] Troll armies, bot networks, and fake news operations are formal structures of misinformation, purposefully built. But to understand how they work, we must go behind the scenes of some of the most engrossing and appalling stories of modern

political intrigue and manipulation, explain the systems behind them, look ahead to how advanced technologies will be
used, and give readers tools to break them down. And ultimately, analyzing these components isn't enough: we need to
know how to fix the problem. So this book concludes by pre-
senting ways that we can protect ourselves and help destroy
the complex lie machines now threatening our democracies.

Most of the investigative journalism around this topic
builds headlines around particular events involving trolls, bots,
or fake news. But these components work very well together.
Trolls launch negative campaigns, usually for radical movements or as paid advertising. They amplify their voice through
automation and social media algorithms. Automated social
media accounts have more impact when they link to fake news.
Fake news has more sophistication and audience appeal when
artificial intelligence is used to manipulate big data about public life. And very soon, the internet of things will generate the
biggest data of all. The *internet of things* is made up of networks of manufactured goods with embedded power supplies,
small sensors, and an address on the internet. Most of these
networked devices are everyday items that are sending and
receiving data about their conditions and our behavior. Such
devices generate massive amounts of data, and if we are not
careful, they could become part of truly enormous mechanisms for social control.

To understand properly how lie machines operate, we
need lots of evidence. From interviews and fieldwork with
political organizations and consultants to big data analysis of
large amounts of content from Twitter and Facebook, we need
to be able to explain how and why these assemblages get built
if we are ever going to work out how to take them apart. So the
analytical effort ahead involves evidence from different countries around the world, expert interviews, and exclusive, rare

data sets sourced from the social media companies themselves. I present original research on government agencies that are spending public money or retasking military units to keep certain hashtags trending, rile up particular groups of people, or defame rising political figures.

The recent slew of surprising political outcomes, strained civic dialogues, and polarizing debates seem—at face value— to be related to social media and the internet. In analyzing a political problem, our first instinct is often to try and identify the one person or factor to pin all the blame on. In the US context, one explanation is that the Russians are responsible for the current political climate because of their interference with how voters deliberated in 2016, 2018, and 2020.[35] A rival theory assigns blame to white supremacists and the far right for successfully using social media to radicalize mainstream conservatives.[36] But both explanations are incomplete because they miss the full perspective of the global political economy behind the lie machines that work on US voters.

How did we get here, and whom do we blame? Is Russia's Vladimir Putin behind it all? Is it our own fault for being addicted to Facebook and Twitter? Unfortunately, the answer is complex, involving both people and technologies in a sensible causal story about how big political lies get produced, distributed, and marketed to us.

The first components that we need to examine are the politicians and governments that generate big lies. As a starting point, we need to track the rise of organized teams of people dedicated to social media manipulation—groups of people often called *trolls*. The first troll armies, which appeared in Russia in 2007, are now organized by the Russian government's Internet Research Agency (IRA). I illustrate how they are used to actively spin government operations and take a close look at the playbook used by social media trolls during a week in which Russia's ruling elites were accused of assassinating a democracy advocate.

The second core component to examine is the distribution method for political lies. We need to scrutinize the automation and algorithms that disseminate misleading political information. What are bots and who makes them? When do people believe a bot, and what impact do bots have on public opinion? I focus on the mechanics of automation on several platforms and on how the mechanism of automating political communication has become more and more sophisticated over the years.

The final components of lie machines to understand are the consultants, marketers, and advertisers who put political lies into a distribution system—and profit by doing so. Many outrageous political stories, rumors, and accusations spread rapidly over social media, and there are businesses that profit by marketing, amplifying, and advertising political lies. In 2016, bots were successful in spreading a crazy story, often called #pizzagate, that supposedly linked Hillary Clinton with a pedophilia ring based out of a pizza parlor in Washington, DC. In 2020, it was automation on TikTok and Twitter that tried to convince local activists and the world at large to dismiss Hong Kong's democracy advocates as violent radicals. Every country now has similar kinds of politically potent lies— stories that remain believed long after they have been disproven. Who takes a potent piece of misinformation that serves the interests of political elites or some ideological agenda, does the market analysis, and unleashes a marketing campaign over social media? Who are the political operatives who buy and sell our data, make or break politicians, and distribute political lies over the internet?

After I've broken the machine down to these components, the next task is to figure out how the parts fit together and affect public life. Understanding the impact and influence of a lie machine means tracing out the flow of information from lie producers through social media distribution systems and marketing plans by professional political consultants. We could call it a case study, archival research, process tracing, or a study of political economy, but it is simpler to say that we need to follow the money.

Lastly, if we can break a lie machine into component parts and then see how the lies and money flow, can we anticipate how such mechanisms might evolve in the years ahead? More importantly, can we catch and disassemble them permanently?

Unfortunately, bots are just early forms of automation that have filled our inboxes and social media feeds with junk. Political chatbots backed by sophisticated machine learning tools are now in development, and these automated accounts provide a much more humanlike, interactive experience. They are not simply scripted bots that can talk about politics. Are you sure we have evolved from primates? Does smoking cause all cancers or just some, and might this connection vary by gender and cigarette brand? There's a chatbot that will make you reconsider such things. Is climate change real? Should we inoculate our kids?

Chatbots have become the hot tool for industry lobbyists seeking to promote junk science. And the next step is to put *artificial intelligence* (AI) algorithms, which simulate learning, reasoning, and classification, behind these bots. Several militaries are looking at ways of using the latest nascent AI personalities and machine learning algorithms for political engagement. Some of the best stories are coming out of China, where closed media platforms allow for large-scale experimentation on public opinion. What can we say now about the political biases in algorithms, and how will AI affect political participation in the democracies?

Most of us are used to experiencing the internet through the browser on our smartphone or computer. But as our cars, refrigerators, and thermostats are also increasingly connected to the internet, how will the data from devices with chips and sensors, wireless radios, and internet addresses be used? What can we learn about political opinion by playing with such big data? Moreover, how will others use this data to coerce us and manage public life? The most basic AI systems are already starting to use complex data to engage real people in political conversations. I highlight some of the amazing ways that this data is being used for meaningful political impact. When sophisticated AI gets to play with big sets of behavioral data from the network devices around us, someone somewhere will attempt to make political inferences from the analysis. Someone will always try to build better lie machines that offer ever more complete systems for understanding our behavior and pushing political opinion. I accept cynicism about the current impact of social media on democracy but not fatalism: civic action and policy leadership may well prevent the worst internet of things scenarios from becoming a reality.

There are multiple challenges before us if we want to live in functional democracies: A politician who doesn't like how a question is phrased dismisses the questioner as "alt-right" or "alt-left." A political leader who doesn't like how a news story is framed labels it "fake news." A political consultant who doesn't like the evidence comes up with "alternative facts." Growing numbers of citizens believe junk science about climate change and public health. Traditional pollsters can't call an election, and the surprising outcomes of elections seem to have their roots in manipulative leaders in other countries.

By closely examining lie machines, we can understand how to take them apart. I offer basic policy recommendations on how we can protect political speech while demolishing the mechanisms for producing, distributing, and marketing misinformation. I provide civic defense tips that should help us proactively protect ourselves in the years ahead. Yet the best way to solve collective problems is with collective action, so I also identify ways that our public agencies can protect us with policies that make it tough for these big lie machines to operate in our democracies. It is possible to block the production, dissemination, and marketing of big political lies, but we'll have to act together to do this effectively.

2

Production

Troll Armies and the Organization of
Misinformation on Social Media

When Russia president Vladimir Putin sponsored a military incursion into Eastern Ukraine in November 2014, he faced immediate criticism from journalists and political opponents at home. The incursion itself was a complex, multimedia operation, with Russian-backed military personnel staging a pro-Russian uprising and actively producing social media content. Within Russia, the opposition was not a significant threat to Putin's control of the government. But over time the opposition to his military aggression grew. At the center of the protests was Boris Nemtsov, and Putin tolerates little dissent.

Nemtsov was a relatively centrist politician who had long been calling public attention to government corruption. He was critical of all the profiteering around government contracts. He argued that destabilizing Ukraine was pointless and costly, and he organized tens of thousands of protesters in peace marches. On February 27, 2015, Nemtsov and his girlfriend were on a date in Moscow. Before midnight, the couple left the restaurant and were ambushed while crossing a bridge near the Kremlin. Nemtsov was shot dead on the spot. Russian courts have since convicted several Chechnyan nationalists for the murder, but the evidence supporting those convictions was weak.

Like an engine, lie machines are built from several components. When all the components are working well, the chances are higher that the machine will successfully manipulate public opinion on an issue. The first component is the process of producing a lie. Organized and motivated people produce lies in the service of some ideology, political candidate, or ruling elite, and the most effective and efficient of such groups can be the agencies of authoritarian governments. Later on, we'll look at other stories and places to understand the other two components—the distribution systems and marketing processes—but one of the earliest assemblages of these parts accompanied Vladimir Putin's invasion of Ukraine, and the crisis around Boris Nemtsov's murder reveals much about how the lie producers operate. Essentially, troll armies are formally organized; they are often paid staff working under contract or in an employment relationship with a government, public agency, or recognized political party. The staff of such social media militias usually have genuine ideological affinities with the ruling elites of a government or party.

Politically motivated murders have become all too common in Russia. Such attacks occasionally involve targets overseas, and when they happen, the Russian government often seems to be ready with a social media strategy for managing the fallout. Common targets include journalists, opposition leaders, and business leaders who don't want to play by the norms and rules of corruption in modern Russia. With Russia's invasion of Ukraine in 2014, the world was closely watching Russia's belligerence, and Nemtsov's murder received international attention. The Russian government's army of social media propagandists at the Internet Research Agency was immediately up and running, and a recently leaked document sheds light on how those propagandists were instructed to spin out stories of Nemtsov's homicide.

The fast pace of international affairs and the negative coverage of Russia in the world's free press means that the Kremlin's media strategy must stay agile and fresh. The government's news agencies, RT (formerly Russia Today) and Sputnik, promote the regime's political perspectives overseas by broadcasting biased news stories and promoting stories of political corruption, racial strife, and social inequality in foreign democracies. A human staff pushes this content across the major social networking platforms; the best available estimate on staff capacity is that the IRA has between four hundred and one thousand paid employees and an annual budget of approximately ten million dollars. These resource commitments allow the Russians to generate media spin quickly in times of crisis.[1]

Guidance from the political center on what messages to distribute comes in the form of a weekly memo on the key issues that staff should be working on and the perspectives they should be taking. The memo doesn't contain specific instructions on what to say and when to say it. It outlines positions and perspectives and makes suggestions about tone and context. On some issues the weekly memo identifies particular lies to propagate, and on others it provides tips on the subtle messaging that makes an issue seem complex, nuanced, and helpfully multifaceted. The guidelines are sent out to the paid army of social-media-savvy staff who then go to work pushing messages out over the thousands of fake user accounts they have set up.

Nemtsov was murdered at 11:30 that night in February

2015, and the Kremlin's social media strategy was immediately ready for action.

The Beginning of Lie Machines

All governments try to shape public opinion, though different regimes do this in varying ways under diverse circumstances. Democratically elected governments tend to do it during military or economic crises, with propaganda offices dedicated to maintaining public support for difficult policies. Such governments, almost by definition, tend to practice censorship and public opinion manipulation on only a select number of critical issues, with oversight by courts or elected officials, and generally not in order to keep leaders in power. In contrast, authoritarian governments regularly use censorship, surveillance, and public opinion manipulation on a wide range of issues and to keep leaders in power.

Wealthy authoritarian governments use their media organizations to shape opinion constantly, but in moments of crisis they intervene aggressively to head off a real confrontation with political challengers or the public at large. Several state bureaucracies, such as Russia and China, have a century of experience managing public opinion through newspapers, radio, films, and television.

The founding story of modern, high-tech lie machines begins with Russia's long-term investments in nationalist youth blogging camps. These teams directed misinformation at Russian citizens over social media using the country's popular LiveJournal blogging system, an effort that involved several government departments. The well-resourced Internet Research Agency came to life in 2012 as a formal organization, with desks, telephones, job ads, and performance bonuses—at least, 2012 is the year that IRA-operated accounts came to life on Twitter.

Political elites in Russia saw how social movements in other parts of the world were using platforms like Facebook and Twitter to organize and decided to apply those same tactics with the aim of political control rather than political change. Effectively, Russia's authoritarian government developed a social media strategy, funded it well, and built the first significant component of the modern lie machine: a professional organization for systematically producing political misinformation specifically for distribution over social media platforms.

These teams, whether operating in the public or private sector, are tasked primarily with manipulating public opinion online: pushing ideology through the algorithms of social media.[2] Over the past decade, several authoritarian regimes have launched such organizations by retasking entire military units to carry out social media manipulation. Even dictators in small countries have begun developing small, professional teams to defend regime policies, attack opponents, and stay alert for moments of crisis. Private firms have sprung up, not just in eastern Europe, but in the world's global cities— boutiques that advertise "social media services" and "political consulting" for any kind of client, be it a government agency, political party, dictator, or candidate campaigning for election. As of 2020, such troll armies operated in seventy countries around the world, with copycat IRA agencies in China, India, Iran, Pakistan, Saudi Arabia, and Venezuela that also generate campaigns targeting users outside their own countries.

Troll armies disseminate computational propaganda over social media platforms using automation, algorithms, and big-data analytics to manipulate public life.[3] Doing this often involves producing junk news stories, spreading them over social media platforms, illegally harvesting data and microprofiling particular citizens, exploiting social media algorithms and putting them into service for influence operations, amplifying hate speech or harmful content through fake accounts or political bots, and producing clickbait content for optimized social media consumption. They are the dictator's response to a social-media-enabled Arab Spring, and they are a standing army to assist with social media spin and manage public perception whenever a dictator stumbles.

What Dictators Learned from the Arab Spring

Many authoritarian regimes began treating social media as a tool for managing public opinion after the events of the Arab Spring. Beginning in late 2010, these popular democracy movements began in Tunisia, inspired democracy advocates in Egypt, and animated other movements to cascade across the region.[4] Governments watched as some of the world's toughest strongmen—Tunisia's Ben Ali, Libya's Muammar Gaddafi, Egypt's Hosni Mubarak, and Yemen's Ali Abdullah Saleh—fell to demands for change despite their many decades in control of public life. Each leader lost power after unparalleled levels of social protest and civil unrest ended their tough regimes. Several other autocrats had to dismiss their cabinets, make political concessions, and redistribute wealth. Discontent cascaded over transnational networks of family and friends to Algeria, Jordan, Lebanon, and Morocco. Several countries remain in crisis today, and in most of these countries it is not clear whether the popular demand for change will result in new sustainable political institutions.

Social protests in the Arab world spread across North Africa and the Middle East largely because digital media allowed communities to realize that they shared grievances and nurtured transportable strategies for mobilizing against dictators. But the early months of the Arab Spring were not about traditional political actors such as unions, political parties, or radical fundamentalists. These protests drew out networks of people, many of whom had not been as successful at political organization before: young entrepreneurs, government workers, women's groups, and the urban middle class.

Ben Ali ruled Tunisia for twenty years, Mubarak reigned in Egypt for thirty years, and Gaddafi held Libya in a tight grip for forty years. Yet their bravest challengers were twenty- and thirty-year-olds without ideological baggage, violent intentions, or clear leadership. The groups that initiated and sustained protests had had few meaningful experiences with public deliberation or voting and little experience with successful protests. However, these young activists were politically disciplined, pragmatic, and collaborative. Even though they had grown up under entrenched authoritarian regimes, they had developed their political identities and aspirations over social media. For several years before the Arab Spring, young people had used social media to learn about political life in countries where faith and freedom coexisted. Then during the Arab Spring, they used social media to express their grievances and coordinate their protests.[5]

Democracy advocates learn tricks from one another, but so do dictators. Authoritarian regimes copy specific policy ideas for public administration and general ways of maintaining legitimacy and control. Research has demonstrated that contact between governments often produces bureaucracies that look alike—they emulate each other's structure and processes. This is particularly true for democracies; such countries are more open about their successes and failures, and public agencies operate with higher expectations for success.[6] However, it is also true of authoritarian regimes that have military units, police units, and national security teams that aggressively learn and apply the tricks that help autocratic regimes stay in power. The most important techniques often involve the machinery of information policy, telecommunications infrastructure, online censorship, and digital surveillance.[7] For some of us, the Arab Spring was an inspiring moment of public demand for regime change. For the affected dictators, it was a lesson in how digital media can be used against them during a power struggle.

We can safely say that since the mid-1990s, digital media has in different ways and contexts been either a necessary or a sufficient cause of social uprising, regime change, and democratization.[8] The Arab Spring exposed, both to researchers and to dictators, several phases of modern social unrest. The first is a preparation phase that involves activists using digital media in creative ways to find one another, build solidarity around shared grievances, and identify collective political goals. The ignition phase that follows involves some inciting incident that is ignored by the mainstream, state-controlled media but that circulates digitally and enrages the public. Second comes a phase of street protests that are coordinated digitally. Next there must be a phase of international buy-in, during which digital media is used to draw in foreign governments, global diasporas, and especially overseas news agencies.

This all culminates in a climax phase in which the state cracks down and protesters are forced to go home (Bahrain, Iran), rulers concede and meet public demands (Egypt, Tunisia), or political groups move into a protracted civil war (Libya, Syria). These days, one mark of the peak of a crisis of social unrest is that the government disconnects the national information infrastructure from the global internet in an attempt to hold back the cascade of unrest. This is the denouement of post-protest information in an ideological war between the winners and losers of the strife.

Having seen this arc of events, dictators began developing their own social media strategies.[9] In the past, authoritarian regimes had easily controlled broadcast media in times of political crisis by destroying newsprint supplies, seizing radio and television stations, and blocking phone calls. It is certainly more difficult to control digital media on a regular basis, but there have been occasions on which states have disabled a range of marginal to significant portions of their national information infrastructure.

Authoritarian governments build lie machines for two broad reasons.[10] The first is to protect political leaders and state institutions from reputational harm. When the results of a rigged election are openly questioned by the public and international actors, social media is used to reassure a domestic audience and restore public trust. Protecting authority can also involve using social media to respond to an internal challenger's propaganda or a neighboring country's meddling in domestic affairs. It can also involve responding to or censoring expressions of dissidence, with the pretense of ensuring national security.

The second common reason regimes give for building out such machinery is the need to preserve public order, cultural values, and the public good. In some cases, authoritarian regimes develop and release computational propaganda to protect social values or religious morals. In others, regimes explain that they need to preserve racial harmony, protect children, or safeguard individual privacy through surveillance, censorship, and computational propaganda. Often the regimes claim that these systems are needed to discourage criminal or destabilizing activity.

Some countries, such as Russia and China, offer many reasons, explanations, and excuses simultaneously or in different combinations depending on the nature of the crisis. Social media platforms have been particularly useful for Russia's ruling elites, who can mix direct attacks on political opponents with public opinion manipulation that helps mislead the entire country.

Some pundits and researchers argue that social media is not part of the complex causal mechanism that explains contemporary social change. This is myopic, however. Perhaps the best evidence that social media is now part of the toolkit for social control is in how many regimes invested in social media communications since the Arab Spring. The same regimes that abused human rights had no problem using Twitter and Facebook to manipulate their citizens. Moreover, these platforms give regimes with significant budgets for psychological operations the ability to work on their own people, on their citizens who have moved overseas, and on the citizens of other countries. As a leader in the use of media control and manipulation, Russia made the first big, creative investments when it put the algorithms of Facebook, Twitter, and Instagram to work in a lie machine.

Training the Trolls

In early 2016, I received a copy of the IRA's social media misinformation strategy for the week of Boris Nemtsov's murder. The document came from an anonymous sender and from a temporary email address. It came encrypted, and after checking it for viruses, I opened it and had it translated. The document has since appeared in a few public repositories and been leaked to several people and organizations.

The document does not prove that Nemtsov's murder

was premeditated by the Kremlin. We can't know if the Kremlin's communications teams had their social media strategy ready to go before the homicide or just reacted instantly to it. But we can conservatively say that the teams had an exceptional capacity to respond swiftly and comprehensively. Boris Nemtsov was murdered just before midnight, and the Kremlin's social media strategy launched just after.

In translation, the document itself is called simply *Assignments for Savushkin 55,* a reference to the physical address of the Kremlin's social media operations building at 55 Savushkin Street in St. Petersburg. The document's metadata—including information about when it was created—contains nothing suspicious. It contained no viruses, and the structure of the content is internally consistent. After a trusted colleague translated the document from Russian into English, another person "back translated" the document with a third individual, turning the English text into Russian and comparing it against the original. This allowed us to check that some of the nuanced rhetoric—always important in political messaging—was accurately translated.

Assignments for Savushkin 55 covers sixty-eight issues that were in the news at the time, ranging from US negotiations with Iran to the status of the South China Sea. It includes economic topics like the exchange value of the ruble and hot-button security issues such as the military maneuvers in Ukraine. Each issue is well researched, with a batch of links to friendly news sources both foreign and domestic.

For each issue there is a basic concept that provides a succinct one-sentence summary of the Kremlin's position. Below that is a list of specific current events—what journalists call *news pegs.* These news pegs are connected to the key themes that the Kremlin wants its social media specialists to reinforce. Next the government researchers provide talking points, which include statements from prominent politicians and public figures about the issue. The researchers provide extensive links to friendly online news sources—and Western ones when those foreign sources seem to support the Kremlin spin. A concluding paragraph summarizes the Kremlin's position, and a helpful list of keywords gives the social media team a set of good hashtags to use.

All of this provides perfect background material for the staff of the Internet Research Agency and a ready supply of photos, links, quotations, and observations to pour into the world's social media feeds. The Kremlin's trolls are trained in how to use these dispatches to push out waves of misinformation.

On February 28, 2015, the primary concern for Russia's trolls was spinning Nemtsov's murder. The spin was simple: the killing didn't obviously serve Putin's interests, so it must have been a foreign provocation.

"There is no doubt that the murder of Boris Nemtsov shocked the public, and especially the opposition," the instructions for that day conclude. "But common sense says the murder would not benefit the government because it would only galvanize the country's anti-government activists." The messaging plan then offers several bizarre, contradictory explanations to be disseminated simultaneously, across both automated and organic accounts, in Russian, English, and Ukrainian.

First, the trolls are instructed to plant the notion that Nemtsov's assassins might have been anti-Russian agents from Ukraine who killed him to disrupt Russian domestic politics. A quote from Putin's press secretary Dmitry Peskov offers speculation about possible causes: "It is obvious that Boris Nemtsov was a member of the opposition, it is obvious that he was in close contact with different people in Kiev, he went there often, it's not a secret, and everyone knows that."[11] Perhaps the Ukrainians killed him?

Second, the trolls are directed to introduce the possibility that the people who organized Nemtsov's murder were also those who shot down Malaysia Airlines Flight 17 the previous summer. "From the political point of view," speculates a senior government official, Ivan Melnikov, "it looks like a brutal, bloody provocation, organized with the same objectives as the Boeing plane crash. Neither first, nor second event were in the interests of the political opponents of Nemtsov." Rhetorically, saying this reinforces the idea that Putin couldn't have ordered either the murder of Nemtsov or the downing of Malaysia Airlines Flight 17 because he wouldn't have benefited from either event. Perhaps there is a multifaceted, international conspiracy against Russia?

Third, the staff trolls speculate that Nemtsov's own opposition supporters might have killed him in an attempt to inspire more antigovernment activism. Government spokesperson Dmitry Olshansky suggests, "Poor Boris Nemtsov was sacrificed in order to revive the opposition. His dead body was supposed to shock people to come out to the streets to direct their anger at the government." He makes the bizarre conclusion that "the murder fits the opposition's desire to escalate domestic tensions." At the time, Russia's own democracy advocates were trying to organize a big demonstration against the government's invasion of Ukraine. Perhaps Putin's opponents murdered their own leader to help energize more protests? The troll army is asked to promote this most unlikely political strategy because even raising the prospect of treachery among Russia's democracy advocates can undermine their moral authority.

With multiple, contradictory messages ready to go within a few hours of Nemtsov's murder, the churn of rumors quickly dissipated public consensus about what, if anything, should be done about his death. The social media campaign of disinformation produced by the IRA's human staff was amplified by almost three thousand highly automated Twitter accounts that all pushed out the same slur at the same time. "Ukrainians killed him . . . . He was stealing one of their girlfriends," they announced in unison.

Of course, an important part of any social media strategy is not just to frame the same incident in multiple ways but to make other incidents seem just as important, insulting, outrageous, or provocative. The messaging instructions for the rest of the week after Nemtsov's murder reveal a lot about how trolls work and what makes them effective.

Throughout that week, Russia's troll armies spoke up on dozens of topics. They discussed the real arrest of a man in Latvia who sympathized with the Russian government and used the arrest to criticize the European record on human rights and freedom of speech. They discussed the Ukrainian government's very real trouble paying Russia for the natural gas needed to heat Ukrainian homes during the cold winter months. This was described as a form of state failure, and they chronicled the desperate attempts of the Russian government to help the Ukrainian economy. Special new military equipment was announced for the troops in the Arctic region. There was a concerted effort to make the ruble seem undervalued. Social media platforms allow the authoritarian regime to track political conversations and the Internet Research Agency to shape and direct such conversations.

Expanding Troll Armies

Over time, the Russian government has developed its internet trolls into a professional army of propagandists.[12] The first well-trained teams of social media trolls were developed in Russia for use against Russians. Many of them were simply "patriotic bloggers" loosely coordinated by ruling elites. But national security services in the country quickly professionalized these teams and tasked them with working on misinformation campaigns across eastern Europe. In short order they needed more staff who could write and speak eloquently in the languages of the region. Significant budgets now provide for hundreds of staff, dedicated workspaces, and performance bonuses. The agency is able to activate campaigns in several countries at once or maintain extended misinformation campaigns outside of elections—such as when Russia was pilloried over the poisoning of Sergei Skripal in a small English town.

The Internet Research Agency now occupies several buildings in St. Petersburg and advertises openly for new recruits. For example, job ads for the Russian troll factory can often be found online. They detail the pay and range of activities for potential new employees: preparation of thematic posts, developing mechanisms to attract new audiences, and monitoring target groups.

The people hired for these positions are chosen for their creativity. Generating politically polarizing content and distributing it in a savvy way over social media takes ingenuity. One example of the content produced by these teams is the campaign to encourage US voters to fear immigration and to abhor the uncertain costs of allowing outsiders into the United States.

One of the most shared cross-platform images known to have come from Russia's Internet Research Agency depicts a downtrodden veteran and suggests that there is a trade-off between assisting veterans or immigrants. "At least 50,000 homeless veterans are starving dying in the streets, but liberals want to invite 620,000 refugees and settle them among us," claims the accompanying text. "We have to take care of our own citizens, and it must be the primary goal for our politicians!"

On its own, this misinformation sets up a false contrast and uses made-up numbers. It uses a reasonable sentiment—that we should take care of our friends and family who do military service—as an ideological accusation against liberals. It is not clear that liberals would want to make this trade-off or even that it is a trade-off. But most importantly, the post lures readers onto websites and additional content that is more sensational, extremist, and conspiratorial.

Perhaps we shouldn't be surprised that an authoritarian government has used a new information technology as a tool of social control and run information operations against its opponents. Perhaps the best evidence of how a comprehensive lie machine can take over a country's public life is Russia itself, where the manipulative strategies have been practiced and perfected on each new social media platform to arrive. In Russia, almost half of all conversation on Twitter is conducted by highly automated accounts. Some of these accounts organically and actively police conversation; others simply generate spam in an effort to make the platform unusable for conversation.[13] The bigger surprise is how rapidly this way of organizing misinformation campaigns has spread globally—even to democracies.

Russia's Troll Army and Political Polarization in the United States

As Russian troll armies became more practiced at using social media algorithms to manipulate public opinion, they got bolder about which country's citizens they would interfere with. With a smooth-running operation, able to handle emergency communications during internal political crises, and some successful experiments working in other languages, Russia's troll armies were next tasked with producing computational propaganda for social media users in the United States.

Russia's Internet Research Agency launched an extended attack on the United States by using computational propaganda to misinform and polarize US voters. What we know about Russia's social media campaigns against voters in democracies comes from the small amounts of data released by the major social media firms.[14] There is certainly a constant flow of examples of suspected Russian-backed, highly automated, or fake social media accounts working to polarize public understanding of important social issues. But understanding the structure and reach of the IRA's efforts requires large pools of data. In the summer of 2017, the major social media firms provided such data to the US Senate Select Committee on Intelligence. The committee then turned to my team and I at Oxford University—the Computational Propaganda Project within the Oxford Internet Institute—to analyze the data.

Major social media firms gave the US Senate and our team data on the accounts that these firms identified as IRA-managed troll and bot accounts. Facebook provided data on ads bought by IRA users on Facebook and Instagram and on organic posts on both platforms generated by accounts that Facebook knew were managed by IRA staff. Twitter provided a vast corpus of detailed account information on the Twitter accounts that the company knew were managed by IRA staff. Google provided images of ads and videos that were uploaded to YouTube.

To analyze the data, we had to commit to a nondisclosure agreement with the US Senate for a short period. This was certainly an impingement on academic freedom, but we decided that our consent was worth it to get an inside peek into how troll armies work. In the end it paid off, and we were able to generate the first, most comprehensive analysis of this rare data, and more importantly, we were able to expose IRA activity across multiple platforms over several years.

The volume of IRA ads and suspicious accounts is small compared to the total number of ads placed and the total user base. But the organic content generated by Russian trolls had enormous reach, with tens of millions of US voters seeing the ads, interacting with fake voters, and sharing the misinformation generated by the IRA. Facebook provided data on 3,393 individual ads. Public data released by the House Permanent Select Committee on Intelligence provided details on 3,517 ads. These ads encouraged users to engage with specific pages. And these pages were the center of issue-based ad campaigns run by the IRA.

Facebook provided data on 76 different advertising accounts that purchased ads on behalf of these campaigns on Instagram and Facebook, though only a handful were responsible for most of the spending on ads. On Facebook, these campaigns generated a total of 67,502 organic posts (produced by the IRA page administrator and not advertised) across 81 distinct pages. On Instagram, these campaigns generated a total of 116,205 organic posts across 133 separate Instagram accounts. The campaigns' organic Facebook posts had very high levels of engagement. In total, IRA posts were shared by users just under 31 million times, were liked almost 39 million times, were reacted to with emojis almost 5.4 million times, and engaged enough users to generate almost 3.5 million comments.

Engagement was not evenly distributed across the 81 pages for which Facebook provided data on organic posting: the top 20 most liked pages received 99 percent of all audience engagement, shares, and likes. Twenty ad campaigns received the most attention from audiences and absorbed most of the IRA's spending. And all the campaigns and pages contained conspiratorial content, polarizing messages, misinformation, simple lies, and other forms of junk news.

On Instagram, a similar pattern is evident. In total, all Instagram posts garnered almost 185 million likes, and users commented about 4 million times. Forty pages received 99 percent of all likes. The themes of these Instagram posts do not seem to differ significantly from those of Facebook, though the presentation style is different. The data Twitter provided contained handles and associated metadata for 3,841 accounts believed to have been managed by the IRA. The analysis of Twitter content in this report covers 8,489,989 posts (tweets, in this case) across 3,822 of these accounts.

The IRA's international activities across the major social media platforms grew significantly after its early successes inside Russia—such as the subterfuge around Boris Nemtsov's murder. In 2016, the average monthly volume of live ads was more than double the 2015 level, and the volume remained similar in 2017. Unlike the ads, the monthly volume of organic Facebook posts rose steadily between 2015 and 2017. Between 2015 and 2016, monthly organic post volume increased almost sevenfold, and it continued to rise rapidly into 2017. On Instagram, after a small increase in average monthly post volume between 2015 and 2016, there was a large increase between 2016 and 2017. Unlike the average volume of Facebooks ads, the average volume of Facebook and Instagram organic posts was much higher in 2017 than in 2016: by a factor of 1.7 for Facebook organic posts, and by a factor of 2.3 for Instagram organic posts. The volume of Twitter posts (tweets) did not change significantly in the years 2015–17.

The Russian secret services bought at least $100,000 worth of ads on Facebook targeting US voters.[15] They used social media to encourage Catalan independence from Spain during a tense national referendum.[16] And as of this writing, several democracies have made criminal indictments, political accusations, and diplomatic complaints against Russia's troll armies.

The Internet Research Agency adapted existing techniques used in digital advertising to spread disinformation and propaganda. They set about creating and managing advertising campaigns on multiple platforms, often making use of false personas or imitating activist groups. This strategy is not a unique invention for politics and foreign intrigue—it is consistent with techniques used in digital marketing.

The overall approach appears to have served three advantages. First, it enabled the IRA to reach its target audiences across multiple platforms and formats. Indeed, the IRA's core messages and target audiences were remarkably consistent across platforms. Second, it helped create a semblance of legitimacy for the false organizations and personas managed by the IRA. We can hypothesize that users were more likely to assume the credibility of the false organizations set up by the IRA because they had a presence across multiple platforms, operating websites, YouTube channels, Facebook pages, Twitter accounts, and even PayPal accounts set up to receive donations. Finally, the IRA was able to leverage its presence on multiple platforms after detection efforts caught up with it by redirecting traffic to platforms where its activities had not been disrupted and by using its accounts on one social media platform to complain about suspensions of its accounts on another platform.

When called to testify before the US Senate in 2018, I was able to report on several stunning findings from our team's analysis of the data.[17] Between 2013 and 2018, the IRA's Facebook, Instagram, and Twitter campaigns reached tens of millions of users in the United States. More than thirty million users, between 2015 and 2017, shared the IRA's Facebook and Instagram posts with their friends and family, liking, reacting to, and commenting on them along the way. Peaks in advertising and organic activity often corresponded to important dates in the US political calendar, crises, and international events. Agency activities focused on the United States began on Twitter in 2013 but quickly evolved into a multiplatform strategy involving Facebook, Instagram, and YouTube, among other platforms.

The most far-reaching IRA activity was in organic posting, not advertisements. In other words, the most pernicious content was not in the political ads simply purchased and placed by Russian agents. It was the seemingly homespun, organic content that had the greatest reach. And that content came from the fake users managed by Russia's troll army.

Russia's IRA activities were designed to polarize the US public and interfere in elections, by campaigning in 2016 for African American voters to boycott elections or to follow the wrong voting procedures. More recently, the IRA campaigned for Mexican American and Hispanic voters to distrust US institutions. Russian trolls have been encouraging extreme right-wing voters to be more confrontational, and they have been spreading sensationalist, conspiratorial, and other forms of junk political news and misinformation to voters across the political spectrum. Surprisingly, these campaigns did not stop once the IRA was caught interfering in the 2016 elections. Engagement rates increased and covered a widening range of public policy issues, national security concerns, and topics pertinent to younger voters. The highest peak of IRA ad volume on Facebook was in April 2017—the month of the Syrian missile strike, the use of the Mother of All Bombs on ISIS tunnels in eastern Afghanistan, and the release of the Trump administration's tax reform plan.

The Internet Research Agency posts on Instagram and Facebook increased substantially after the US elections of 2016, with Instagram seeing the greatest increase in IRA activity. The IRA accounts actively engaged with disinformation and practices common to Russian trolling. Some posts referred to Russian troll factories that flooded online conversations with posts; others denied being Russian trolls. When they faced account suspension, some trolls complained about the political bias of platforms.

Perhaps least surprising, but most important, is that IRA misinformation activities bloomed at key moments in US public life. Troll armies plan for and campaign around moments of political crisis and election year milestones. Broadly, over the years 2015–17, the volume of activity in Facebook ads, Facebook posts, and Instagram posts increased from the Democratic and Republican National Conventions in July 2016 to voting day in November 2016. But several spikes in ad and post volume happened around the dates of important political events, in particular:

- the third Democratic primary debate and the sixth Republican primary debate (both in January 2016);
- the presidential candidate debates between Hillary Clinton and Donald Trump (autumn 2016);
- election day (November 8, 2016); and
- the dates of the postelection Russian hacking investigation (December 29 and 30, 2016).

The data on Russia's Internet Research Agency provided to the Senate Select Committee on Intelligence by social media and internet platforms demonstrates a sustained effort to manipulate the US public and undermine its democracy. With years of experience of manipulating public opinion in Russia, the IRA used major social media platforms, including Facebook, Instagram, and Twitter, to target US voters and polarize US social media users.

The Russian effort targeted many kinds of communities within the United States, but especially the most extreme conservatives and those with particular sensitivities to race and immigration. The IRA used a variety of fake accounts to infiltrate political discussion in liberal and conservative communities, including African American activist communities, in order to exacerbate social divisions and influence the agenda. Accounts posing as liberal and as conservative US users were frequently created and operated from the same computers.

The Social Organization of Misinformation

Social media is a ubiquitous and prominent part of everyday life, and users place high amounts of trust in these platforms. Indeed, even after several years of scandal, polling still finds that people trust technology companies more than public services, food and drink companies, pharmaceutical firms, banks, oil and gas companies, the news media, and government (in order of diminishing trust).[18] With the ability to segment audiences and target messages in a quick, cheap, and largely unregulated way, these platforms have not surprisingly attracted the interest of political operators. Unfortunately, there is mounting evidence that social media is being used to manipulate and deceive the voting public—and to undermine democracies and degrade public life.

It is difficult to tell the history of social media or anticipate its future without understanding trolls. If the history of the internet is the history of spam, the history of social media is similarly intertwined with the history of trolls.[19] In politics and public life, social media conversations are inflected by political rants with idiosyncratic spelling, invitations to join small groups of resisters, truthers, and woke individuals. Political campaigns come with pleas to back your moral outrage by sharing content with your social network and donating to the cause. As Finn Brunton explains in *Spam,* all this activity is shaped by many different programmers, con artists, bots and their botmasters, pharmaceutical merchants, marketers, identity thieves, crooked bankers and their victims, cops, lawyers, network security professionals, vigilantes, and hackers. But it is much harder to filter out organic political trolling, which tends to be dynamic and conversational and is produced by organizations with significant budgets and personnel.

It may not be surprising that an authoritarian government would develop techniques for manipulating public life over new media. The Russian origins of modern lie machines—algorithms carrying ideology—won't be surprising to experts in the long history of propaganda. Political elites in every country work hard to manage public perception and grievances. And there is a long history of governments meddling in each other's domestic politics, promoting local politicians who favor foreign interests, and even interfering in how a country runs its elections. But the use of direct messaging and personal engagement with voters in strategically important districts in the West caught many other analysts off guard.

Unfortunately, the trolling techniques pioneered by the Russian government have spread far and wide. Prominent politicians and lobbyists in every country—authoritarian or democratic, and at all levels of government—use them.[20]

The successes of these enormous lie machines cannot simply be attributed to resourcing and organizational behavior. Social media firms themselves provided the algorithms—the toolkit—and explaining the current challenges to public life would be incomplete without including the technical part of this sociotechnical system.

The machine driving politics has itself changed. Public life, going forward, will be fundamentally different from what has gone before because of the purposeful coordination of vast amounts of misinformation that can be passed across networks of family and friends. The politics of the future, and the now, is different from what came before. And if we don't act quickly, political life will be perpetually dominated by these lie machines.

Lie machines, however, are not just produced by authoritarian governments to oppress their own populations through misinformation and disinformation. A close look at Russia's troll armies reveals a lot about the production side of a modern lie machine. But we can look to other examples, in other countries, to illustrate best how the distribution and marketing of big political lies works.

3
Distribution
Deceitful Robots and Politics in Code

In the summer of 2017, a group of young political activists in the United Kingdom figured out how to use a popular dating app to attract new supporters. They understood how the dating platform Tinder worked. They knew how its algorithms distributed content, and they were familiar with the platform's culture. So the campaigners built a bot. The bot engaged with real people on Tinder, and though the conversations started as flirty, they soon turned political—and to the strengths of the Labour Party.[1]

The bot accounts sent between thirty thousand and forty thousand messages in all, targeting eighteen- to twenty-five-year-olds in constituencies where the Labour candidates needed help.[2] It is always hard to tell how many votes are won through social media campaigns. In this case, however, the Labour Party either won or successfully defended some of these targeted districts by just a few votes. In celebrating their victory over Twitter, campaign managers thanked their team—their team of bots.

We know that social media are among the internet's most

used applications. In the United States, 85 percent of adults regularly use the internet, and 80 percent of those people are on Facebook.[3] Most of the time such apps are not used for politics. But as social platforms have become increasingly embedded in people's lives—they are so perfectly designed for segmenting and targeting messaging, so quick and cheap and unregulated, and so trusted by users—it's obvious that they wouldn't be ignored by political operators for long. There is mounting evidence that social media is being used to manipulate and deceive voters—and to degrade public life.

We once celebrated the fact that social media allowed us to express ourselves, share content, and personalize our media consumption. It is certainly difficult to tell the story of the Arab Spring without explaining how social media platforms allowed democracy advocates to coordinate themselves in surprising new ways and to send their inspiring calls for political change cascading across North Africa and the Middle East.[4] But the absence of human editors in our news feeds also makes it easy for political actors to manipulate social networks. In Russia, some 50 percent of Twitter conversations involve highly automated accounts that communicate with humans and one another. In October 2019, as protests against China's authoritarian control over Hong Kong disrupted the ruling party's celebrations of seventy years in power, complex algorithms scanned for images of protest and pleas for help, removing them from social media.[5]

Such automated accounts and social media algorithms can distribute vast quantities of political content very quickly or can be scripted to interact with people in political debates. Professional trolls and bots have been aggressively used in Brazil during three presidential campaigns, one presidential impeachment campaign, and the race for mayor of Rio.[6] We've found political leaders in many young democracies actively using automation to spread misinformation and junk news. In the United States, we have found that misinformation on national security issues was targeted at military personnel on active duty and that junk news was concentrated in swing states during the presidential election of 2016.[7] It seems that social media has gone from being the natural infrastructure on which to share collective grievances and coordinate civic engagement to being the medium of choice for crafty political consultants and unapologetic dictators.[8]

Political Automata

In fact, social media platforms might be the most important tools in the trolling toolkit. It is the algorithms for automation that allow a single person with a corrupted message to disseminate nonsense and spin to large numbers of people. To understand lie machines, we must understand automation and algorithms that disseminate misleading political information. What are social media bots and how do they work? When are they used and who uses them?

A *bot* or *botnet*—from *robot* and *network*—is a collection of programs that communicate across multiple devices to perform tasks. A single bot can be a fake user with preprogrammed statements and responses that it serves up to its immediate network. A collection of bots, working in concert as a botnet, can generate massive cascades of content for an extended network of human users. Their tasks can be simple and annoying, like generating spam. Or they can be aggressive and malicious, like choking off internet exchange points, promoting political messages, and launching denial-of-service attacks. Some programs simply amuse their creators; others support criminal enterprises.[9] On social media platforms, botnets can be an important part of a lie machine because they can take a politically valuable falsehood and distribute it to large numbers of carefully selected users. Bots on Twitter or Tinder, or highly automated accounts on Facebook and Instagram, can rapidly deceive large numbers of people using networks that both humans and bots have co-created. Sometimes the deceit is in pushing misinformation around. In the case of the bot on the Tinder dating platform, the deception was in using automation to flirt and divert human users into political conversations.

In my book *Pax Technica,* I wrote about how bots and fake social media accounts threaten public life. People naturally tend to trust friends, and many still trust technology. With the power to replicate themselves and rapidly send messages, bots can quickly clutter a conversation in a network of users or slow down a platform's servers and eat up a user's bandwidth. Another, more pernicious problem is that bots can pass as real people in our social networks. It is already hard to protect your own online identity and verify someone else's, and bots introduce an additional level of uncertainty about the interactions we have on social media.

Badly designed bots can produce the typos and spelling mistakes that reveal authorship by someone who does not quite speak the native language. Well-designed bots blend into a conversation. They may even use socially accepted spelling mistakes, or slang words that aren't in a dictionary but are in the community idiom. By blending into our social networks, they can be a powerful tool for negative campaigning—emphasizing and exaggerating a political opponent's flaws.[10]

Indeed, political communication strategies involving bots share many features with what is often called *push polling.* Both are insidious forms of automated, negative campaigning that plant misinformation and doubt with citizens under the pretense of running an opinion poll. For example, an ad might invite you to participate in an informal survey about political leaders, but the survey questions may be full of misleading information carefully crafted to make you dislike one particular leader or policy option. Survey researchers have long known that you can shape how people answer a question by priming them through word choice and limited answer options. Push polls exploit those effects by purposefully biasing the polling questions. In fact, a user's responses are rarely analyzed by the campaign putting out the survey—collecting meaningful data is secondary to planting seeds of doubt, stoking fears, or enraging respondents through politically motivated lies.

The American Association of Public Opinion Researchers has produced a well-crafted statement about why push polls are bad for political discourse, and many of the complaints about negative campaigning apply to bots as well. Bots work by abusing the trust people have in the information sources in their networks.

It can be very difficult to differentiate feedback from a distant member of your social network and automatically generated content. Just because a post includes negative information or is an ad hominem attack does not mean that it was generated by a bot. But just as with push polls, there are some ways to identify a highly automated account:

- one or only a few posts are made, all about a single issue;
- the posts are all strongly negative, over-the-top positive, or obviously irrelevant;
- it is difficult to find links to and photos of real people or organizations behind the post;
- no answers, or evasive answers, are given in response to questions about the post or source; and
- the exact wording of the post comes from several accounts, all of which appear to have many of the same followers.

Bots have influence precisely because they appear to be a genuinely interactive person with a political voice. Such highly automated accounts seem to have personality, though they may not always identify their political sympathies in obvious ways. Interaction involves questions, jokes, and retorts, not simply parroting the same message over and over again. Message pacing is revealing: a legitimate user can't generate a message every few seconds for extended periods.

Highly automated accounts and fake users generating content over a popular social network abuse the public's trust. They gain user attention under false pretenses by taking advantage of the goodwill people have toward the vibrant social life on the network. When disguised as people, bots can propagate negative messages that may seem to come from friends, family, or others in your extended network. Bots distort issues or push negative images of political candidates to influence public opinion. They go beyond the ethical boundaries of political polling by bombarding voters with distorted or even false statements to manufacture negative attitudes. By definition, political actors engage in advocacy and canvassing of some kind or other. But distributing misinformation with highly automated accounts does not improve civic engagement.

Bots are this century's version of push polling, and they may have even more dire consequences for public understanding of social issues. In democracies, they can interfere with political communication by helping political campaigns coordinate in ways that they are not supposed to, they can illegally solicit contributions and votes, or they can violate rules on political disclosure.[11] Later on, we will explore a push poll campaign run during the Brexit debate in the United Kingdom, algorithmically distributed to the users who were most likely to respond to its prompts.

Social bots are particularly prevalent on Twitter. These computer-generated programs post messages of their own accord. Often social bot profiles lack rich and meaningful account information, and the content they produce can seem disconnected and simple. Whereas human social media users get access from front-end websites, bots access such websites directly through code-to-code connection, through the site's wide-open application programming interface, posting and parsing information in real time.

Bots are versatile, cheap to produce, and ever evolving. They can be designed for any social media platform, live and thrive in the cloud, produce content, interact at any hour of the day, and replicate themselves. Indeed, for several years now, unscrupulous internet users have deployed bots for more than such mundane commercial tasks as spamming or scraping sites like eBay for bargains. Unfortunately, the unscrupulous internet users are often dictators and desperate political campaign managers.

But do bots have influence? Researchers have been largely unable to provide statistical models to show how a particular social media post may change an individual voter's mind—although the social media firms themselves have those models. Firms like Facebook, Twitter, and Google don't share data with that level of granularity with researchers, but within the firms such models help inform their pricing strategies for advertisements. Still, three forms of evidence reveal that bots have influence. First, we have the dictators and political professionals themselves, many of whom sink significant resources into bot-driven campaigns and argue that their campaigns have influence. Second, we understand the process by which a message that disseminates across networks of bot accounts crosses a threshold into human networks. Third, we can measure the long-term damage to public understanding caused by campaigns that have relied on bots to distribute misinformation on a massive scale.

Cry "Havoc!" and Let Slip the Bots of War

If you can't comprehensively surveil or censor social media, the next best strategy is to write automated scripts that clog traffic, promulgate your message, and overwhelm the infrastructure of your political enemies.[12] One unique feature of the emerging political order is that it is being built, from the ground up, for surveillance and information warfare. Another is that it has new kinds of soldiers, defenders, and combatants.

For example, the ongoing civil war in Syria has cost hundreds of thousands of lives. The great majority of these are victims of President Bashar al-Assad's troops and security services. After the Arab Spring arrived in Syria, it looked as if the forces loyal to the Ba'ath government would stay in control. Speedy military responses to activist organizations, torturing opposition leaders and their families, and the use of chemical weapons seemed to give Assad the strategic advantage. Yet despite these brutal ground tactics, he could not quell the uprising in his country. And by 2013 he was losing the battle for public opinion, domestically and abroad. Even China and Russia, backers that supplied arms and prevented consensus in the United Nations Security Council about what to do, appeared to succumb to political pressure to join the consensus that Assad had to go.

What's unusual about the crisis is that it might be the first civil war in which bots actively participated from the beginning, with serious political consequences. Public protest against the rule of Assad, whose family had been in charge since 1971, began in the southwestern Syrian city of Daraa in March 2011. Barely a month later, Twitter bots were detected trying to spin the news coming out of a country in crisis. In digital networks, bots behave like human writers and editors.

People program bots to push messages around or to respond in a certain way when they detect another message. Bots can move quickly, they can generate immense amounts of content, and they can choke off a conversation in seconds. From early on, people in Syria and around the world relied on Twitter to follow the fast-moving events. Journalists, politicians, and the interested public used the hashtag #Syria to follow the protest developments and the deadly government crackdown.

The countering bot strategy, crafted by security services loyal to the government, had several components. First, security services created a host of new Twitter accounts. Syria watchers called these users "eggs" because at the time, users that didn't offer a profile photo were represented by a default symbol of an egg. No real person had bothered to upload an image and personalize the account. Regular users suspected that these profiles were bots because most people do put an image up when they create their profiles. Leaving the default image in can be the marker of an automated process, since bots don't care what they look like. These eggs followed the human users who were exchanging information on Syrian events. The eggs generated lots of nasty messages for anyone who used keywords that signaled sympathy with activists.

Eggs swore at anyone who voiced affinity for the plight of protesters and antigovernment forces, and eggs pushed pro-regime ideas and content that had nothing to do with the crisis. Eggs provided links to Syrian television soap operas, lines of Syrian poetry, and sports scores from Syrian soccer clubs to drown out any conversation about the crisis. One account, @LovelySyria, simply provided tourist information. Because of how quickly they work, the pro-regime bots started to choke off the #Syria hashtag, making it less and less useful for getting news and information from the ground.

Investigation revealed that the bots originated in Bahrain, from a company called Eghna Development and Support.[13] This is one of a growing cluster of businesses offering so-called political campaign solutions in countries around the world. In the West, such companies consult with political leaders seeking office and lobbying groups who want some piece of legislation passed or blocked. In authoritarian countries, political consulting can mean working for dictators who need to launder their images or control the news spin on brutal repression. Eghna's website touted the @LovelySyria bot as one of its most successful creations because it built a community of people who supposedly just admire the beauty of the Syrian countryside; the company has denied directly working for the Syrian government.[14]

At the beginning of the Syrian civil war, when @Lovely Syria went to work, it had few followers and little online community presence. With two tweets a minute, @LovelySyria was prevented by Twitter itself from devaluing a socially important hashtag. Of course, automated scripts are not the only source of computational propaganda. The Citizen Lab and Telecommix found that Syrian opposition networks had been infected by a malware version of a censorship circumvention tool called Freegate.[15] So instead of being protected from surveillance, opposition groups were exposed to it. And a social media campaign by a duplicitous cleric was cataloging his supporters for the government.

In today's physical battlefield, information technologies are already key weapons and primary targets. Smashing your opponent's computers is not just an antipropaganda strategy, and tracking people through their mobile phones is not just a

passive surveillance technique. Increasingly, the modern battlefield is not even a physical territory. And it's not just the
front page of the newspaper either. The modern battlefield involves millions of individual instructions designed to hobble
an enemy's computers through cyberwar, long-distance strikes
through drones, and coordinated battles to which only bots
can respond.

More recently, bots have gone after the aid workers hop-
ing to assist in the complex humanitarian disaster that has
evolved in Syria.[16] Officially known as the Syria Civil Defence,
at its peak this organization, also known as the White Helmets,
had some 3,400 volunteers—former teachers, engineers, tai-
lors, and firefighters—who would rush into conflict zones to
provide aid. The organization has been credited for saving the
lives of thousands of people, but a successful campaign driven
by Russian bot networks spread rumors that the group was
linked to Al-Qaeda. This turned the organization's volunteers
into military targets. The Syrian government accused Syria
Civil Defence of exaggerating claims that they were being attacked and charged the group with causing the damage themselves. Eventually, many group members had to be rescued and
resettled well away from conflict zones.

Over time this political campaign industry has grown,
with firms competing to offer increasingly aggressive services.
Until it filed for bankruptcy, Cambridge Analytica offered clients services ranging from data mining and potent negative
campaign strategies to political entrapment and bribery.[17] In
2016 the Trump campaign solicited proposals from the now-
defunct Israeli firm Psy-Group for campaign services, and the
company pitched the idea of creating five thousand fake social
media users to swing party supporters his way and of using
social media to expose or amplify division among rival campaigns and factions. The proposal used code names for Donald

Trump ("Lion"), who was the potential client, and the target, Ted Cruz ("Bear"), who was a rival for the Republican Party's nomination as a presidential candidate.[18]

Firms promising to use big-data analytics to make political inferences emerged in the early 2000s.[19] So when social media applications took off, the ability to use the algorithms themselves to study and then push opinion quickly became a specialized craft within the political consulting industry. It isn't always easy to evaluate whether firms like Cambridge Analytica and Psy-Group can make good on their promises. But as Mark Andrejevic observes in his book *Infoglut,* the core of the promise is that specialized analytics software and big data can let such neuromarketers understand what people are really thinking, at a nuanced level beyond what any pollster or seasoned political analyst can reveal.

Bot Spotting

Understanding precisely how social media platforms affect public life is difficult. Even the social media platforms themselves seem to have trouble reporting on the depth and character of the changes they have brought about in society. When evaluating how the Russian government contributed to the Trump campaign in the lead-up to the 2016 US presidential election, Facebook first reported that this foreign interference was negligible. Then it was reported as minimal, with just three thousand ads costing $100,000 linked to some 470 accounts that were eventually shut down.[20] But as public and political pressure to understand the election grew, so did the company's estimates of the electoral impact of other social media platforms caught up in the fray. Under questioning from US congressional investigators, the lawyers from these companies revealed that Russia's propaganda machine had in fact reached

126 million Facebook users with this ad campaign. Foreign agents had published more than 131,000 messages from 36,000 Twitter accounts and uploaded over a thousand videos to Google's YouTube service.[21]

What makes social media a powerful tool for propaganda is obviously its networked structure. Such platforms are distributed systems of users without editors to control the production and circulation of content—but also no editors to help with quality control and be responsible for content.

In its prepared remarks sent to Congress, Facebook stated that the Internet Research Agency, the shadowy Russian company linked to the Kremlin, had posted roughly 80,000 pieces of divisive content that were shown to about twenty-nine million US users between January 2015 and August 2017.[22] Those posts were then liked, shared, and followed by others, spreading the messages to tens of millions more. In its statement, Facebook also said that it had found and deleted more than 170 suspicious accounts on its photo-sharing app Instagram and that those accounts had posted around 120,000 pieces of Russia-linked content. Each account was designed to present itself as a real social media user, a real neighbor, a real voter.

Since the US election in November 2016, and with increasing scrutiny of foreign influence by Congress, the Federal Bureau of Investigation, and the world's media, platforms like Facebook and Twitter have been more aggressive in shutting down highly automated accounts and the profiles of fake or abusive users. They maintain that they have no role in facilitating foreign interference in elections or degrading public life in democracy. They insist that they are not publishing platforms with responsibility for what is disseminated to their users. But in almost every election, political crisis, and complex humanitarian disaster, their algorithms disseminate misinformation.

Can democracy survive such computationally sophisticated political propaganda?

What Is Computational Propaganda?

Simply defined, *computational propaganda* is the misleading news and information, algorithmically generated and distributed, that ends up in your social media feed. It can come from networks of highly automated Twitter accounts or fake users on Facebook. It can respond to your flirtation with a political entreaty. Often the people running these campaigns find ways to game the news feeds so that social media algorithms exaggerate the perceived importance of some junk news. But sometimes they simply pay for advertising and take advantage of the services that social media companies offer to all kinds of advertisers. The political campaigns or foreign governments that generate computational propaganda experiment with all manner of platforms, not just Instagram and YouTube. Doing so usually means breaking terms of service agreements, violating community norms, and using platform affordances in a way that engineers didn't intend. Sometimes it means also breaking election guidelines, privacy standards, consumer protection rules, or democratic norms. Unfortunately, not all of these things are always illegal or fully investigated and prosecuted.[23]

Generating computational propaganda usually requires that someone compose the negative campaign messages and attack ads for automated and strategic distribution. Social media firms provide the algorithms that allow for automating the distribution of messages to targeted users. For example, geolocation data from mobile phones helped Facebook compute where ad placement would be most effective, sending more of the Brexit campaign ads to users in England rather than Wales or Scotland. During the 2016 elections in the United States, junk news was concentrated in swing states. Essentially, social media firms provide the computational services that allow for the most effective distribution of misinformation. The precise computational work of ad auction systems varies from platform to platform, but all are designed to automate the process of converting insights about users into compelling ads, delivered to the users most likely to react as desired.

Tracing Bot Networks

When we independent researchers trace these bot networks, we are constrained because we can anticipate only some of the hashtags that will be used in an election campaign. Candidate names, party names, and a handful of other standard words are often useful keywords that help analysts identify posts, tweets, or ads about politics. Of course, this means that we'll miss political conversations that are not tagged this way as well as conversations hashed with unusual terms and terms that emerge organically during a campaign. Nonetheless, once we identify a network of highly automated accounts, we try to answer a few basic questions so that we can compare trends across countries. Which candidates are getting the most social media traffic? How much of that traffic comes from highly automated accounts? What sources of political news and information are used?

Investigating how automation is used in political processes usually means starting off with a handful of accounts that are behaving badly. They might, for example, produce such high volumes of content that they effectively choke off a public conversation. Or they might push small amounts of content, but from extremist, conspiratorial, or sensationalist sources. There are many ways to track bots at scale, but all have weaknesses. Bots tend to follow other bots. They produce content that is often found to come from other accounts, word for word and character for character. But we have found that the best way to manage false positives on Twitter—no humans like being called bots—is simply to watch the frequency of contribution. We have found that accounts tweeting more than fifty times a day using a political hashtag are invariably bots or high-frequency accounts mixing automated techniques with occasional human curation. This varies somewhat from country to country. But few humans—even among journalists and politicians—can consistently generate fresh tweets on political hashtags for days on end.

Not surprisingly, given how important and complex this problem is, the study of computational propaganda has grown by leaps and bounds in recent years. With support from the National Science Foundation and the European Research Council, our team of social and computer scientists has been tracking automated activity on social media platforms, how misinformation spreads across these networks, and ultimately how this might affect democracy itself.

The 2016 US presidential election certainly stands as a watershed moment for understanding the evolution of computational techniques for spreading political propaganda across online social networks. In the most public way possible, it demonstrated how the algorithms used by social media companies to spread influence can be turned into tools for political interference—plowshares turned into swords. Both candidates attracted networks of automated Twitter accounts that pushed around their content during the election period.

For example, mapping political conversations by tracking the most prominent Clinton-related, Trump-related, and politically neutral hashtags revealed that the Trump-supporting bot networks were more active and expansive than the Clinton-supporting ones. There were more of them, they generated more content, and they were more interconnected.

Even though bots are simply bits of software that can be used to automate and scale up repetitive processes (such as following, linking, replying, and tagging on social media), we can still see evidence of the human deliberation behind the strategic use of bots for political communication. A bot may be able to pump out thousands of pro-candidate tweets a day, giving the impression of a groundswell of support, confusing online conversation, and overwhelming the opposition—but that bot was coded and released by a human.

The use of automated accounts was deliberate and strategic throughout the 2016 election season, seen most clearly with the pro-Trump campaigners and programmers who carefully adjusted the timing of automated content production during the debates, strategically colonized Clinton-related hashtags by using them for anti-Clinton messages, and then quickly disabled these activities after election day. We collected several samples of Twitter traffic and mapped the botnets by extracting the largest undirected, connected component of retweets by bots within the set of either Trump-related or Clinton-related hashtags. We tracked political conversations on Twitter during the three presidential debates and then again in the ten days before voting day. Following these trends over time allowed us to examine how social media algorithms could be leveraged in political strategy.

First, we demonstrated that highly automated bot campaigns were strategically timed to affect how social media users perceived political events. After the first and second debates, highly automated accounts supporting both sides tweeted about their favored candidate's victory in the televised debates. We also noticed campaigners releasing bot activity earlier and earlier with each debate night. Some highly automated pro-

Trump accounts were declaring Trump the winner of the third debate before the debate was even broadcast.[24]

Second, we saw that, over time, the pro-Trump bot networks colonized Clinton's community hashtags. For the most part, each candidate's human and bot fans used the hashtags associated with their favorite candidate. By election day, around a fifth of the exclusively pro-Trump Twitter conversation was generated by highly automated accounts, as was around a tenth of the exclusively pro-Clinton Twitter conversation. The proportion of highly automated Twitter activity rose to a full quarter when we looked at mixtures of Clinton and Trump hashtags—often seeing the negative messages generated by Trump's campaigners (#benghazi, #CrookedHillary, #lockherup) injected into the stream of positive messages being traded by Clinton supporters (#Clinton, #hillarysupporter).

Last, we noticed that most of the bots went into hibernation immediately following the election: their job was done. Bots often have a clear rhythm of content production. If they are designed to repeat and replicate content in interaction with humans, then their rhythm of production follows our human patterns of being awake in the day and asleep at night. If they are frontloaded with content and just push out announcements and statements constantly, then they can run twenty-four hours a day, building up an enormous production volume over time. These highly automated accounts certainly worked hard during the campaign season—but interestingly, they were programmed to wind down afterward. Whoever was behind them turned them off after voting day.

The data consists of approximately 17 million unique tweets and 1,798,127 unique users, collected November 1–11, 2016. The election was on November 8, 2016. To model whether humans retweeted bots, we constructed a version of the retweeting network that included connections only where a human user retweeted a bot. The result was a directed retweet network, where a connection represented a human retweeting a bot. Overall, this network consisted of 15,904 humans and 695 bots. On average, a human shared information supplied by a bot five times. The largest coherent Trump botnet captured in a sample of Twitter traffic consisted of 944 pro-Trump bots, compared with the 264 that supported Clinton.

The largest botnet we found in our sample of the Trump supporter network was more than three times the size of the largest network of highly automated accounts promoting Clinton. Moreover, in comparing these networks, we found that the highly automated accounts supporting Trump were much more likely to be following each other. This suggests that the organization of Clinton's network of highly automated accounts may have been a little more organic, with individual users creating bots and linking up to networks of human accounts in a haphazard way. In contrast, Trump's retweeting network was quite purposefully constructed, and highly coordinated and automated accounts were a much more prominent feature of the Twitter traffic about Trump.[25]

Misinformation over other platforms spread in similar ways. Facebook's algorithms distributed false news stories favoring Trump thirty million times and distributed false news stories favoring Clinton eight million times.[26] Only some 14 percent of US voters thought of social media as their most important source of election news. The average voter saw, on average, only one or two fake news stories, and only half of those voters who recalled seeing fake news stories believed them. However, evaluating averages like this isn't the best way to understand the impact of algorithmic content distribution, and a few percentage points in exposure can result in major political outcomes. The national averages may seem low, but these fake news stories were concentrated in swing states, where voters would have been exposed to much higher volumes of misinformation and where a few percentage points of change in voter opinion gave Trump the edge in claiming victory for the entire state.[27]

Social media platforms have responded to mounting criticism from government and civil society with modest initiatives. They occasionally catch a large volume of fake users and have introduced small interface changes to combat the spread of malicious automation. But the problem has gone global. The flow of political conversations has always been directed by information infrastructure, whether newspapers, radio, or television. But the degree to which algorithms and automation speed up the flow of political content—and widen its distribution—is entirely new. And these computational techniques have spread globally with exceptional speed. Usually it takes only a few campaign cycles for political consultants to take the latest dirty tricks around the world.

Programmers and political campaign managers have devised a wide range of applications for bots in political communication. It is often hard to attribute responsibility for bot activity on social media platforms. Some platforms thrive because of permissive automation policies, and political campaign managers take advantage of such supportive algorithms. Other platforms require that bot accounts identify as such or require that only real human users can create profiles. But creative political consultants find the work-arounds, even if they have to violate a platform's terms of service, pay for custom programming, or hire trolls to generate messages.

At this point we've seen bots used in multiple ways. Obviously, they can be used by one candidate to attack another candidate in a seemingly public conversation. They can be used to plant false stories, debate with campaign staff, and argue with opponents. They can be used to make a candidate look more popular, either by inflating the numbers of followers or boosting the counts of attention received (likes, retweets). They can be used to apply all the negative campaigning techniques that campaign managers use on other media, such as push polling, rumor mongering, or direct trolling.

Candidates have used bots to encourage the public to register complaints against other candidates with elections officials. For example, during the US Republican primary elections, highly automated accounts managed by a Trump advocate encouraged voters to complain about another candidate's campaign practices to the Federal Communications Commission. The complaint concerned Senator Ted Cruz's use of robocalls—automated phone calls that remind voters to vote or conduct push polling. So bots were used to encourage humans to complain about bots bothering humans. Similarly, the political consulting firm New Knowledge experimented with a bot network that would advocate for a conservative candidate, but then get caught and outed as a Russian-backed support campaign. This would have made it look as if the Russians were campaigning for the conservative and embarrassed the conservative candidate—except that the whole effort was exposed.[28]

Political Bots from around the World

When our research team tried to inventory global spending on computational propaganda, we were surprised to find organized and coordinated ventures in every country we looked at, including many Western democracies. The earliest reports of organized social media manipulation emerged in 2010, and by 2017 we found details on such organizations in twenty-eight countries. By 2018 formal misinformation operations were in play in forty-eight countries, with some half a billion US dollars budgeted for research and development in public opinion manipulation. When we took an inventory in 2019, there were seventy countries with some domestic experience in cyber-troop activity, and eight countries with dedicated teams meddling in the affairs of their neighbors through social media misinformation.

Looking across these countries, we found evidence of every authoritarian regime in our sample targeting its own population with social media campaigns and several of them targeting foreign publics. But authoritarian regimes are not the only—or even the best—organizations doing social media manipulation. In contrast, for democracies it was their own political parties that excelled at using social media to target domestic voters. Indeed, the earliest reports of government involvement in nudging public opinion involve democracies, and new innovations in political communication technologies often come from political parties and are trialed during high-profile elections. Cyber troops can work within a government ministry, such as Vietnam's Hanoi Propaganda and Education Department, or Venezuela's Communication Ministry.[29] In the United Kingdom, cyber troops can be found across a variety of government ministries and functions, including the military (Seventy-Seventh Brigade) and electronic communications (Government Communications Headquarters, or GCHQ). Most democracies can't hide the fact that they have such groups, though they will be secretive about group activities.[30] And in China, the public administration behind cyber troop activities is incredibly vast. There are many local offices that coordinate with their regional and national counterparts to create and disseminate a common narrative of events across the country.[31] In other nations, cyber troops are employed under the executive branch of government. For example, in Argentina and Ecuador, cyber troop activities have been linked to the office of the president.[32]

In our comparative analysis, we found several patterns in how different kinds of countries organize cyber troops. In democracies, strategic communication firms generally enter into contracts with political parties to manipulate voters or agreements with government agencies to shape public opinion overseas. In authoritarian regimes, cyber troops are often military units that experiment with manipulating public opinion over social media networks. In other words, social media companies have provided the platform and algorithms that allow social control by ruling elites, political parties, and lobbyists.

Many governments have been strengthening their cyberwarfare capabilities for both defensive and offensive purposes. In addition, political parties worldwide have begun using bots to manipulate public opinion, choke off debate, and muddy political issues.

The use of political bots varies across regime types and has changed over time. In 2014, my colleagues and I collected information on a handful of high-profile cases of bot usage and found that political bots tended to be used for distinct purposes during three events: elections, political scandals, and national security crises. The function of bots during these situations extends from the nefarious practice of demobilizing political opposition followers to the relatively innocuous task of padding political candidates' social media follower lists. Bots are also used to drown out oppositional or marginal voices, halt protest, and relay false messages of governmental support. Political actors use them in broad attempts to sway public opinion.

Elections and national security crises are sensitive moments for countries. But for ruling elites, the risk of being caught manipulating public opinion is not as serious as the threat of having public opinion turn against them. While bot-nets have been actively tracked for several years, their use in political campaigning, crisis management, and counterinsur-gency has greatly expanded recently. A few years ago, it was tough for users to distinguish between text content made by a fully automated script from that produced by a human. Now video can be computationally produced, so that familiar na-tional leaders can appear to say things they never said and political events that never occurred appear to be captured in a recording.

In a recent Canadian election, one-fifth of the Twitter followers of the country's leading political figures were bots. All the people running for US president in 2020 have bots fol-lowing their social media accounts, though we can never know whether this is a deliberate strategy by candidates to look more popular or an attempt by opponents to make them look bad. We know that authoritarian governments in Azerbaijan, Rus-sia, and Venezuela use bots. The governments of Bahrain, China, Syria, Iran, and Venezuela have used bots as part of their attacks on domestic democracy advocates.

Pro-Chinese bots have clogged Twitter conversations about the conflict in Tibet and have meddled in Taiwanese politics.[33] In Mexico's recent presidential election, all the major political parties ran campaign bots on Twitter. Furthermore, the Chinese, Iranian, Russian, and Venezuelan governments employ their own social media experts and pay small amounts of money to large numbers of people to generate progovern-ment messages.

Even democracies have groups like the United Kingdom's Joint Threat Intelligence Group. These secretive organizations are similarly charged with manipulating public opinion over social media using automated scripts. Sometimes Western governments are unabashed about using social media for political manipulation. For example, the US Agency for International Development tried to seed a "Cuban Twitter" that would gain lots of followers through sports and entertainment coverage and then release political messages by using bots.[34]

The Syrian Electronic Army is a hacker network that supports the Syrian government. The group developed a botnet that generates proregime content with the aim of flooding the Syrian revolution hashtags—such as #Syria, #Hama, and #Daraa—and overwhelming the prorevolution discussion on Twitter and other social media portals. As the Syrian blogger Anas Qtiesh writes, "These accounts were believed to be manned by Syrian Mokhabarat (intelligence) agents with poor command of both written Arabic and English, and an endless arsenal of bite and insults."[35] Differing forms of bot-generated computational propaganda have been deployed in dozens of countries.[36] Contemporary political crises in Thailand and Turkey, as well as the ongoing situation in Ukraine, are giving rise to computational propaganda. Politicians in those countries have been using bots to torment their opponents, muddle political conversations, and misdirect debate.

The Market for Robots

Although I have mostly discussed Twitter, every platform has processes that can be automated by someone who wants to distribute massive amounts of political content. At first, it was mostly authoritarian governments that used bots, but these days they are also a part of most major political campaigns in democracies.

Between 5 and 15 percent of all Twitter accounts are either bots or highly automated accounts; two-thirds of the links to information about news and current events shared on Twitter come from bot accounts; and in 2018, Twitter swept out seventy million fake accounts.[37] By 2020, Twitter was regularly culling bot accounts in advance of every nation's elections. Most of these crafty bots generate inane commentary and try to sell stuff, but some are given political tasks.

The reason that digital technologies are now crucial for the management of political conflict and competition is that they respond quickly. Brain scientists find that it takes 650 milliseconds for a chess grandmaster to realize that her king has been put in check after a move. Any attack faster than that and bots have the strategic advantage—they spot the move and calibrate the response in even less time. The most advanced bots battle it out in financial markets, where fractions of a second can mean millions in profit or loss. In competitive trading they have the advantage of being responsive. Slight changes in information or social validation from a few humans, however, can result in a massive cascade of misinformation. Such changes or validation can drive social media algorithms to treat the content as socially valuable, distributing it even more widely.

Bots do have a role in managing traffic on digital networks, whether electronic stock markets or social media feeds. Bots help make transactions speedy and help filter the political news and information we want from that we don't want. And they don't always capture our attention. They can certainly compete for it, clog our networks, stifle economic productivity, and block useful exchanges of information, though. Elsewhere, I've argued that we are living in a *pax technica* because the majority of the cultural, political, and economic life of most people is managed over digital media.[38] Having control of that information infrastructure—whether it's by technology firms, dictators, or bots—means having enormous power.

A lie machine is constituted by the relationships among devices, bots, and social media accounts as much as by the relationships among real people. Obviously, technology networks grow along with social networks, but that means that our digital devices and social media accounts increasingly contain our political, economic, and cultural lives. These user identities provide some significant capacities but also some troubling constraints on our political learning.

Occasionally, bots and other automated scripts are used for social good. Citizens and civic groups are beginning to use bots, drones, and embedded sensors for their own proactive projects. Such projects, for example, use device networks to bear witness, publicize events, produce policy-relevant research, and attract new members.

It certainly takes a dedicated organization of people to construct and maintain a socially significant lie. But social media firms provide the platforms that can be used to distribute such content in a massive way. And this technology for distributing it is incredibly fast—in a sense, it automates lying. We will soon discuss how to assemble the different parts: the human trolls, combined with the bots described here, are components of a larger mechanism that can involve high-volume, high-frequency content production for particular communities with highly partisan content.

Even campaign managers admit that they are importing tactics from authoritarian regimes into democracies. As Patrick Ruffini, a Republican research and analytics firm founder, told *Politico*, "A lot of these unsavory tactics that you would see in international elections are being imported to the US."[39]

The market for deceitful robots is a competitive one. The people who build and maintain such networks must create visually pleasing and sufficiently entertaining stories of political intrigue, hidden agendas, or malfeasance. The stories must contain enough realism about the situation that users accept the claims enough to click through, read more, and retain a few details and doubts. The story must be delivered by a relatively enclosed network of other accounts and other content that affirms and reinforces what people are seeing.

Now that we understand how social media algorithms are used by modern lobbyists, politicians, and foreign governments to disseminate information, we next need to examine the process of marketing a political lie.

4

Marketing

Junk News Operations and News We Shouldn't Use

Warm coconut water is not a cure for cancer. Yet a basic internet search returns results that are more qualified and suggestive than they should be, with websites pointing to one specific research report that links a chemical found in coconut water (and many other foods) to the death of cancer cells that were artificially created within rat stomachs.[1] And search engine links to things "people also ask" include information that doesn't offer the focused answer to the question of whether coconut milk can cure cancer: No. So it is concerning when misinformation about coconut water as a cure for cancer spread rapidly among India's social media users in 2019.[2] Some health misinformation might just be the result of a lone miscreant. Yet we have detected politically motivated health misinformation—notably with Russian origins—about fake cancer cures, the health risks of 5G cellular technology, and or campaigns to promote homeopathy or naturopathy campaigns over health science.[3] Encouraging your opponent's citizens to consider homeopathy over medical science serves a broad political goal of weakening them by demeaning evidence and encouraging their irrationality.

Russia's Internet Research Agency pioneered many of the social media tricks we now see plied on voters in democracies. They first practiced these on their own citizens and those living in eastern Europe. I experienced one of the first of the great social media misinformation campaigns in the summer of 2014. I was living in Budapest, and that summer, Russian-backed troops shot down Malaysian Airlines Flight 17 over Ukraine. Much of Europe was on high alert because of the open conflict in Ukraine, and people in eastern Europe were particularly anxious about what the Russian government might try next. My Hungarian friends noticed several kinds of conspiracy theories coming from social media about the plane crash. Russia's neighbors were on high alert, too, wary of potential spillover effects and political consequences of active military maneuvers in their area.

My friends received dozens of different messages about Flight 17 over social media ranging from wrong to ridiculous. One story was that Ukraine's democracy advocates had shot the plane down, because they thought Vladimir Putin was on board. Another story said that the US military had shot it down, mistaking it for a Russian military plane. My favorite story explained that a tank crew from World War II—which had been lost in the great forests of Ukraine for seventy years—emerged, saw the plane, and shot it down.

It was clear to me that there was an underlying structure to all the stories, which came through public and private Facebook pages, and they all seemed to diverge equally from the emerging facts of the incident as reported in more recognized, trustworthy news outlets. Most appeared to be news stories from outlets that no one had heard of before the incident. The

lies came in the form of ads that were formatted like news stories, or as stories promoted by the platforms in a news feed, or
as links shared by casual acquaintances or distant family. No
one story dominated. My Hungarian friends didn't believe any
of them and simply joked about the most absurd ones. But the
effect on public conversation was real: everyone was uncertain
about what had happened, everybody had a different story they
thought was closest to the truth, and nobody had a single story
that they could respond to or act on. I could not tell if these
rumors were produced in a coordinated way, but the outcomes
were consistent.

Organizing Junk News

In 2016, Twitter bots and fake Facebook accounts were successful in spreading a story, often via the hashtag #pizzagate,
linking Hillary Clinton with a supposed pedophilia ring operating from a pizza parlor in Washington, DC. The story was
debunked well before voting day in the United States, but even
a month afterwards, pollsters found that more than a quarter
of adults surveyed were either certain that Clinton was connected to the child sex ring or that some part of the story must
have been true. Of the people who had voted for Trump, almost half either thought it was true or weren't sure one way
or another.[4] When asked about the evidence for this claim—a
month after voting day—a surprising number of adults believed
that evidence of some kind did exist. When the *Economist*
asked if "leaked email from some of Hillary Clinton's campaign staffers contained code words for pedophilia, human
trafficking and satanic ritual abuse"—what we now refer to as
Pizzagate—more than a third of respondents (38 percent)
thought that this was true or probably true.[5] Three months
after the election, a quarter of voters still believed President

Trump's unsupported claims—made well before voting day—of widespread voter fraud.[6]

We have now discussed how political bots work, using some unique examples of entirely automated networks of Twitter accounts that manage to push significant volumes of content on to networks of humans. Understanding how highly automated social media accounts operate is just the beginning, however. What makes botnets powerful is not so much their stealth, the quality of their legends, their speed, or the volume of the content they pump into a political conversation. It's the quality of the political lies, the images, videos, and rhetoric that can shape public understanding of social problems and potential solutions. Moreover, it takes an efficient and persistent delivery system of bots and compelling, well-crafted content to make a lasting impact. We will do a deep dive into the mechanics of such a campaign in the next chapter. But before that, we need to examine the organizations that do all the marketing around big political lies and the people who do such work as a career.

The long-term causes and effects of junk news and misinformation campaigns are a global problem. During the 2016 Brexit debate in the United Kingdom, the Vote Leave campaign announced that the country would save £350 million a week—money that would be put toward public health care. The country's statistics authority said that the number was wrong. Months later, the people behind the campaign admitted that the number had been made up. But the false claim helped the Vote Leave campaign win popular support. In the days before the Brexit referendum, nearly half the public believed the claim to be true. There was widespread disbelief in forecasts coming out of the Treasury office, and public sentiment suddenly shifted ten points toward an inclination to leave the European Union.

Such junk news stories are parts of structured campaigns of misinformation, rapidly scaled and released as part of a strategic junk news operation. They are formally produced and distributed by well-resourced organizations, staffed by people who can combine the craft of smart rhetoric with the algorithms of social media firms. In particular, in countries such as the United States, there are additional communities of tech-savvy, politically disaffected alt-rightists who use social media to manipulate journalists and mainstream media outlets.[7]

There is a long history to fake news production, but in the past, it was mostly used in times of war and crisis. Today it is used to help get legislation passed and to help keep social elites in power. It helps promote junk science that threatens public life in many ways. And there are firms that do this work as professional political consultants.

When my research team broke the global story of how these false stories were being circulated and how the distribution systems worked, we called the stuff *fake news* because the bulk of it was simply made up. It wasn't real news: the stories never happened, the pictures were doctored, and the statements quoted were never said. But as we dug into the phenomenon of misleading content packaged to look like news, we found that it wasn't just that the facts were wrong. We found content in which most of the facts were correct but the conclusions didn't make sense. We found articles in which a few facts were accurate but the bulk of the writing was commentary and opinion writing—not news reporting. Moreover, we had no way of knowing how much fact checking had gone into a piece of writing, whether the publisher was *Russia Today* (now RT) or the *New York Times*. We could compare the sources of political news and information and could assess the professional norms of journalism across organizations. So instead of thinking of this content as fake news, we labeled it *junk news,* which allowed us to track the full range of conspiratorial, sensationalist, extremist, and factually incorrect political news and information.

We are learning more about how junk news organizations work and what they produce. And it turns out there is interesting diversity in how they operate. Sometimes they look like newsrooms. Sometimes they evolve out of military units that have been retasked with manipulating public opinion. In day-to-day operations, their organizational behavior usually mimics that of a tech start-up or telemarketing firm.

Imitacja Consulting

One such firm operates from Warsaw, Poland. Over the past decade, it has developed fake political identities and seeded them across many social media platforms.[8] One of the company's executives spoke to us, on conditions of anonymity and the use of pseudonyms for himself and the company's name. Nonetheless, Daedalus was willing to show off the organization—which here I call Imitacja Consulting—and to talk about how they affect public life.[9]

Imitacja Consulting was founded within months of Facebook's arrival in Poland, and some of the company's best legends have been running since 2006. In social media terms, a *legend* is the biographical background, supported by a stream of photos, comments, and online activity, that makes an account appear to represent a genuinely social, real person. In the past decade, the firm has created more than forty thousand unique identities, each with multiple accounts on various social media platforms and portals. These identities use unique internet addresses so that technically, as the controller uses the profile, the fake person consistently appears to be from the same part of the world and doesn't betray an association with the other profiles. Imitacja's controllers fill a legend's social

media accounts with content and interact with real users. Posting stories, liking and sharing content from real users, and
joining online groups make the accounts seem to belong to
real, active people. Over time, the company's stable of forty
thousand legends has been used to create a network of several
hundred thousand fake legends across multiple platforms to
interact with citizens around the world.[10]

Politics isn't the core of Daedalus's business, however,
and Imitacja Consulting's main clients aren't politicians. The
company's legends are primarily rented out to private sector
clients from the pharmaceuticals or natural resources industries. They certainly do get calls from political candidates, political parties, and political campaign managers during elections, but for the months in between major elections, the client
base consists of regular firms seeking social media advertising
or industry lobbyists who wish to run a political campaign on
a single issue.

As with any other kind of media campaign, the company's sales team works with the client to outline strategic objects for an exciting "word of mouth" or "guerrilla marketing"
campaign. If fresh legends are needed, the sales team will have
controllers create them, starting with a new email address
through a free email provider such as Google or Yandex. Using
this invented name, new email address, and a prepaid mobile
phone number, the team creates accounts on many kinds of
social media platforms and services. The controllers pull photos off the internet, modifying them slightly so that they will
be harder for fraud detection algorithms to identify. The controller starts building a commentary history on different sites
and services around the web. With a few product reviews on
Amazon, a few reactions to news articles, some photos on Instagram, and some videos posted to YouTube, a casual user
would see a credible human moving around the internet.[11]

Each controller manages a dozen legends at a time, with each legend having a coherent writing style, interests, and personality. Controllers use a virtual private network to spoof internet addresses so that their accounts leave a digital trail of relevant and associated metadata about the country where they seek influence. If the legend is from Seattle, that user will appear to log in from different locations around the city and from some regular and predictable internet addresses—just like a user who regularly works from a home or an office. When it is time to put the legends to work for a client, the controller crafts unique content, never copying and pasting across legends. This makes it difficult for social media firms to look for shared content and identify the network of legends. As the legends start posting to Facebook groups and Instagram accounts, it is very difficult for another user, researcher, or even the company itself to identify the fake users. According to the executive at Imitacja Consulting, even if a legend starts to look suspicious, all these tricks make it very difficult for Facebook, Twitter, or any of the other platforms to be *certain* that the legend is not a real person.[12] Access to these human-curated, fake users is a premium service, costing much more than it would simply to rent botnets.

This organization provides a level of deniability for the client, who may not even know exactly (and probably does not want to know) what specific techniques are being used by its marketing consultants. Furthermore, subcontracting with Imitacja is a low-risk endeavor: although these ways of marketing content violate many platforms' service terms, they may not break the law. If a firm takes the precautions, it is unlikely that this activity will ever be exposed, and if it is, it is not clear how either the firm or its clients would be held legally accountable. Creating new fake accounts is a manual task, although Imitacja Consulting has experimented with automating various steps of the account-creation process. Indeed, Daedalus argues that his firm has carved out a special niche for itself. Whereas other consultants use automation and manipulate social media algorithms to take over or redirect particular political conversations, his legends are used to persuade in a more subtle manner.[13]

Outlining his firm's broader strategy, Daedalus argues that the company's trolls and bots do not attempt to influence public opinion by going directly to voters. Rather, the firm's strategy is to target "opinion leaders," including journalists, politicians, bloggers, and key activists. By infiltrating influential WhatsApp groups, mining comment sections, and directly striking up conversations with these opinion leaders, the goal is to try to convince the targets that their wider network sincerely believes in Imitacja's campaign by providing long-term nudges.

The amount of labor and attention that goes into some efforts is staggering, and the most involved campaigns will involve several Imitacja employees merging their networks of accounts to stage and steer conversations on social media. An entire thread on such a platform can feature dozens of fake accounts all posing as engaged citizens, down-voting unsympathetic points of view and steering a conversation in the service of some ideological agenda—a key activity in what has come to be known as political *astroturfing*.[14] Ordinary people who log onto these forums may believe that they are receiving a legitimate signal of public opinion on a topic when they are in effect being fed a narrative by a secret marketing campaign.

Although the current public concern is mostly about automated bots, Imitacja believes that bots' uses are limited because they cannot interact with real users in a sophisticated manner. From what we've learned in our interviews, political bots that try to affect discussion directly are highly inelegant and almost certain to be discovered. Since a client must never be linked to these fake accounts, Imitacja uses bots only in moments of crisis: for spamming political targets, rapidly spreading messages of hate, fear, or anger, and distracting or misleading public attention from a problem. Such highly automated accounts used need not be sophisticated as they are not designed to persuade but rather to spam and perhaps to influence platform algorithms. Bots that retweet a negative story about a political figure, for example, can spread it widely by helping it trend on Twitter. They could try to discredit another candidate by building a network of obvious bots that would pose as that candidate's followers, spamming forums and harassing others in the name of another candidate to make it seem as if the rival candidate was employing bots and trolls.

Imitação Services

Around the world, these social media consulting firms have a pretty consistent organizational form, a remarkably similar business model, and a standardized set of service offerings, regardless of the political environment in which they operate. In Brazil, the firm of what I will call Imitação Services has worked for politicians of many stripes, as well as lobbyists pulling the levers of government on numerous issues.[15] Not only does the company take on politicians as clients, but it actively generated computational propaganda in Brazil during the 2014 presidential elections, the impeachment of former president Dilma Rousseff in 2016, the 2016 municipal elections in Rio de Janeiro, and the 2018 presidential elections that put Jair Bolsonaro in office. Like many democracies, Brazil had no laws to guide the use of computational propaganda during elections. So innovative firms like Imitação Services figured out how to put bots and trolls to work for clients interested in promoting a wide range of economic and political ideas or wishing to meddle in the country's ongoing debates about corruption, privatization, and social reform.[16]

One estimate by ComScore, a global marketing and data analysis firm, suggests that Brazilian users spend over 95 percent of their social media time on Facebook.[17] As in almost every country in the world, traditional corporate media networks are being overtaken by the internet, and more informal, alternative information sources are spreading through social networks, email, personal messaging systems, or other online means. Facebook is by far the dominant social network, with applications like WhatsApp, Instagram, Skype, Twitter, and LinkedIn used by different people in different ways across countries. YouTube is almost as popular as Facebook as a social network, but in terms of time spent, Facebook is the overwhelming favorite.[18]

Imitação Services organizes its staff the same way its Polish counterpart does. One staff member, Roberto, earns $360 (£270) each month running twenty legends that create buzz around the company's clients on Facebook and Twitter. This organization and its rival firms in Brazil can price out the cost of "likes" from their fake Brazilian users on a platform such as Facebook. The company Brasil Liker, for example, sells likes for Facebook pages at $1.50 for fifty and $59 for three thousand. For full posts, clients pay $26 for ten thousand.[19]

The industry as a whole got a lot of bad press when a memorandum from Brazilian president Dilma Rousseff's campaign was leaked to the press after her 2014 election.[20] The memo covered the use of bots during the campaign, asserting that opposing candidate Aécio Neves's operation used them not only on Twitter and Facebook but on WhatsApp and that it spent an estimated $2.9 million in purchasing and deploying these within the social networks and private messaging applications.

Even with a handful of rivals, Imitação dominates the market in Brazil. The firm started off by boosting the popularity of a new presidential candidate on Twitter during nationally televised debates in 2014.[21] Occasionally someone tries to sue the firm, or elections officials apply fines. After Imitação's 2014 foray into presidential politics, a rival political campaign urged Brazilian regulators to fine the company, and the electoral law was amended in 2015 to restrict such "electoral propaganda" on the internet and specifically on social networks.[22] Yet the penalties rarely add up to much, and sometimes the publicity is good for business.

One of Imitação's employees we interviewed, Maria, was an expert on the use of bots in Brazilian political campaigns. She stated that the political marketing industry involved fun and inspiring work because of the energy and creativity required to remain competitive, stay ahead of the law, and adapt to new platforms: "One always has to run ahead of these innovations in communications that are evolving, faster all the time. Each election you have a new law about campaigns. It is very dynamic. You make a new regulation or new law, and six months later a new technology is developed which can frustrate the system. There is also the problem of private networks such as WhatsApp, where there is no way to monitor them."[23] Once in office, most politicians don't wish to divest themselves from their astroturf following. And losing candidates often want to try again later, becoming Imitação clients, too. Sometimes the political consultants involved in the winning campaign go off and start their own consulting firm, offering access to the same tools and tricks that were used by or against them.

Some of Imitação's rivals were involved in the impeachment campaign that brought down President Rousseff. Fake users on Facebook and Twitter bots greatly amplified calls for her resignation, making it seem—in very short order—as if there was a mass movement with an energized consensus around a clear demand. And of course, the appearance of such a political movement drew in more human protesters and real voters. The issues of corruption in the presidency were real, and the struggling economy contributed to Rousseff's early end. Yet there is no doubt that social networks played a key role in developing this narrative and organizing the protests. Within the online landscape, bots had played a role from the beginning, and they never stopped in their electronic opposition to her administration, possibly a key factor in the speed of her defenestration. Bots and fake users certainly had a role in the recent 2018 elections, with new evidence that WhatsApp had become an important platform for spreading junk news.[24]

Maria also described a new kind of application developed for the 2016 mayoral race in Rio. A supporter could donate his or her social capital by giving the candidate's campaign access to real social network accounts. This software would allow a candidate to like and share content from within the supporter's personal profile—effectively handing account control over to the political consultants. For a three-month period, the supporter's user ID and password would sit with the campaign, and the consultants would control the user's political activities. Maria suggested that this tool was often offered to only one political party and argued that it was decisive for that party's electoral victories in many municipalities.[25]

One such local battle pitted Marcelo Crivella, the right-wing leader of an evangelical megachurch, against Marcelo Freixo, a state representative, professor, and member of the left-wing Socialism and Liberty Party, in the final round. Both candidates accused each other of spreading online rumors and complained about rampant fake news stories to elections authorities and in public debates. One story falsely claimed that

Crivella would privatize public parks and charge people to enter them. Another wrongly claimed that Freixo would legalize marijuana and abortion. Both candidates created websites to denounce these rumors, and Freixo began a legal action against Crivella.[26] Freixo had less exposure on television, so he took to using WhatsApp, an encrypted messaging service where there were no rules against the spread of false information.[27]

Imitação strategists noticed that social activity was moving to all sorts of new platforms, including Instagram, Tinder, and Signal. They realized that people were migrating away from Facebook because these new platforms had better affordances—users could more effectively control group membership and communicate more securely. Imitação strategists decided that to stay competitive as a business, their legends also had to have profiles on those platforms. It was easy for their fake users to be invited to join these trusted groups on smaller platforms. In fact, Imitação's founders reasoned, their fake users would probably have more influence over the smaller networks on secured and specialized platforms where trust runs high than on open public platforms such as Twitter and Facebook. Imitação also gathered public opinion data for clients by sending users to join groups on encrypted platforms like WhatsApp and Telegram.

Fake user accounts can have a big impact in large democracies like Brazil, where there are lots of political parties, many elections and varied levels of government, and a highly mobile population. Such fragmentation makes it easier to exploit smaller communities of like-minded thinkers, and the smallest political rumors and misinformation campaigns can be enough for Imitação to bring protesters into the streets or discredit a political candidate. Obviously Imitação didn't always seed political polarization, but the firm certainly exacerbated it and profited from it.

Disinformation as a Day Job

It was tough to get to know these firms. Organizations like these, or Russia's famous Internet Research Agency, must ultimately rely on a staff of hundreds who maintain hundreds of thousands of social media profiles. Sometimes the operation consists of loose affiliations of small specialized businesses and freelance workers who live near one another.[28] They try to keep company secrets, but big disinformation campaigns are run by people working day jobs—not by lone programmers with a political grudge or an ideological passion. Like many jobs, these positions come with pay scales, performance bonuses, organizational hierarchies, office politics, and paperwork to fill out. If a country's misinformation industry is well developed, these jobs are openly advertised.

Understanding junk news from the point of marketing is important because it takes us beyond rhetorical features and exposes the purpose of such content. What defines junk news is not so much its use of logical fallacies, doctored images, and extremist, sensationalist, or conspiratorial content. It is the strategic use, for political and ideological purposes, of commentary masking as news and the placement of such commentary in social media feeds with users' own data about social association, cognitive bias, and behavioral metrics. Thus the masking is twofold: the organizations that produce, disseminate, and market junk news are well hidden from voters, elections officials, and sometimes even the political candidates themselves. The content produced is political commentary presented, consumed, and circulated as if it is professionally produced journalism.

Indeed, this planning care provides some plausible deniability to Poland's Imitacja Consulting and Brazil's Imitação Services. Often Imitacja is a subcontractor to a subcontractor, providing "social media optimization" to a firm specializing in "political strategy consulting" that itself is just contracted to even bigger public communications firms. Clients don't want full written records about what subcontractors do. Such details might become public knowledge and get clients in trouble with elections officials or the courts.

My contacts in businesses like these can rarely point to clear evidence that the accounts they control influence election outcomes, and political campaign managers don't always tell their candidates what firms have been hired to help with the campaign. But in political battles it is now a normal campaign strategy to employ some communications experts to use social media algorithms and automation to amplify a political voice.

These firms reveal much about how computational propaganda works and why both firms and the propaganda are a threat to democracy. First, these consultants expose weaknesses in how we manage elections. Some laws are out of date or are not enforced, and not all political leaders or policy makers understand how lie machines work. Second, they demonstrate how modern campaigns connect various social networks in a coherent strategy, using WhatsApp groups to drive people to more public forums on places like Facebook and Twitter. Third, it appears that the amount of money required to create large social groups and massive streams of content while engaging users across platforms is small relative to the size of the potential impact—it's a profitable business. Finally, social media propaganda campaigns persist beyond the formal limits of the election, often in contravention of electoral law, and after the end of the election day itself. Just as the internet allows campaigns to reach people in more personal ways than candidates and parties can do in an age of mass media governed by television, newspapers, and radio, so it also allows political actors to continue to pursue their political objectives through computational or traditional propaganda beyond conventional limits.[29]

In countries as different as Poland and Brazil, the junk news industry has had a long-term, negative impact on public life. The information environment has become particularly polarized, mirroring events happening at the same time in places like the United States and Europe.[30] Researchers at the University of São Paulo surveyed attitudes of 571 protesters at the April 2015 demonstrations and found that they either did not trust any of the major political parties or trusted them very little.[31] The effects of fake news were also apparent: 64 percent of respondents thought that the ruling party wanted to create a communist regime, and 53 percent thought that a drug gang was standing in as an armed wing of the party. Mirroring Donald Trump's accusations about fake voting in the United States, 43 percent believed that the party had brought fifty thousand illegal Haitian immigrants into Brazil to vote in the 2014 elections. Months later, at a protest supporting Rousseff, the researchers found that 57 percent believed that the United States had fomented protests against corruption to get at Brazil's oil, and 56 percent believed that the judge leading the massive Lava Jato corruption case, Sérgio Moro, had deep loyalties to one of the political parties.[32] These facts were demonstrably false but were widely shared on social media.[33] Moreover, now that the industry is well developed in both countries, some firms are able to take on international contracts, to influence what people in other countries think about politics and public policy.

Two Countries, Same Junk

On voting day in a democracy, junk political news and information like this should not be marketed to citizens. Compared to serious news organizations, firms like Imitacja and Imitação get poor grades for professionalism, style, credibility, bias, and producing counterfeit political news and information.

In terms of professionalism, these outlets do not employ the standards and best practices of professional journalism. They refrain from providing clear information about real authors, editors, publishers, and owners. They lack even basic transparency and accountability information about their funding models and do not publish corrections on debunked information. Stylistically, they use emotionally driven language with emotive expressions, hyperbole, ad hominem attacks, misleading headlines, excessive capitalization, unsafe generalizations and fallacies, moving images, graphic pictures, and mobilizing memes. They lack credibility, relying on strategically employed false information and conspiracy theories. They report without consulting multiple sources and do not employ fact-checking methods. Sources themselves are rarely trustworthy or balanced.

The bias of these outlets runs from a slight ideological perspective to hyperpartisan reporting. They frequently present opinion writing and commentary essays as news. Finally, these organizations often produce counterfeit news sites, mimicking the colors and branding of professional news media. They counterfeit fonts, branding, and stylistic content strategies. Such commentary is disguised as news, with references to news agencies and credible sources, and headlines are written in a news tone, with bylines, a date, and stamps for time and location.

Over the past couple of years, our team at Oxford University has been examining the distribution of poor-quality political news and information across social networks. We have found that people in the United States share more junk news than people in other advanced democracies such as France,

Germany, and the United Kingdom. We have demonstrated that junk news was concentrated in swing states during the 2016 US presidential election. More recently, we have found that social media campaigns were targeting US military personnel and veterans and their families with misinformation on national security issues. We've found junk news being marketed, with different amounts of success, in national elections in India, Mexico, and a dozen countries across Europe. We've found it being marketed during political crises in Hong Kong and Cairo. Even when the public is paying close attention to current events, elections around the world have meant lucrative contracts for firms like Imitacja and Imitação because political parties want to be sure to turn that attention into votes.

Social media has become an important source of news and information in most democracies. An increasing number of users consider platforms such as Twitter and Facebook sources of news. At important moments of political and military crises, social media users not only share substantial amounts of professional news but—sometimes unknowingly—share the extremist, sensationalist, conspiratorial, and other junk news that has been marketed to them.

Why Are We Susceptible to Junk News?

The design and implementation of social media platforms has put several advanced democracies into a kind of democratic deficit. Social media algorithms allow fake news stories from untrustworthy sources to spread like wildfire across networks of family and friends. The platforms provide a very real structure to what political scientists often call *elective affinity* or *selective exposure*. At their core, both concepts simply mean that we prefer to strengthen our ties to the people, information sources, and organizations we already know and like.

Although algorithms and advertisements filter and deliver information, users also select what they want to see or ignore. Scholars have emphasized the important role that individuals play in exercising their information preferences on the internet. Online friend networks often perform a social filtering of content, which diminishes the diversity of information that users are exposed to. Academic studies have demonstrated that people are more likely to share information with their social networks that conforms to their existing beliefs, deepening ideological differences between individuals and groups.[34] As a result, voters do not get a representative, balanced, or accurate selection of news and information during an election, nor is the distribution of important information randomly distributed across a voting population. Research on selective exposure shows that people select traditional media and broadcasting sources that they wish to be exposed to and that they choose to associate with groups of voters, community associations, political parties, and candidates. However, it is not clear that selective exposure works in quite the same way on the internet. Studies of selective exposure on social media have not reached the same level of consensus that researchers working on broadcast media have reached.[35]

The selective exposure theory argues that most voters prefer messages that support rather than conflict with their beliefs and world view. These kinds of messages increase voters' confidence that they are thinking, feeling, and acting in a correct or acceptable manner, that they have made good decisions about information quality in the past, and that they need not consider radical shifts in political affiliation. Effectively, selective exposure helps explain why there are very few mass defections from political parties or experienced political candidates. As early as 1964, researchers at Columbia University investigated how voters picked up political news and information, finding that people tend to expose themselves selectively to their pre-ferred candidate's messages.[36] Since then, almost every study of the subject has affirmed some selective exposure effects.

What might explain why people selectively expose them-selves to political news and information? The partisanship ex-planation suggests that people pay attention to political con-tent that fits the ideological package they already subscribe to. If they've already expressed a preference for a particular can-didate, they will select messages that strengthen, not weaken, that preference.[37] Effectively, this means that voters tend not to change political parties or favored candidates because they are unlikely—voluntarily or proactively—to acquire radically new information that challenges their perspectives and under-mines their preferences. Obviously, the more interested a voter is in a subject, the greater the likelihood of such selective at-tention.[38]

A second explanation for selective exposure focuses on one's *schemata*—cognitive representations of generic concepts with consistent attributes that can be applied to new relation-ships and new kinds of information.[39] Whereas the partisan-ship explanation emphasizes deference to already preferred political figures and groups, the schemata explanation empha-sizes that we take cognitive shortcuts and depend on ready-made prior knowledge.[40] According to this explanation, in-formation itself has a gatekeeping role, such that we rely on the things we already know and believe rather than learn the science and facts that are relevant to each new policy issue.

A third possibility is that we rely on selective exposure because we don't want to face the cognitive dissonance of ex-posure to radically new and challenging information.[41] There is minimal research into this explanation, but there is some evidence that if we have to face cognitive dissonance, we work hard to construct a consistent explanation and reward ourselves when we are successful in doing so. For example, in an experiment in which US Democrats were presented with a prominent Democratic politician's inconsistent remarks, and US Republicans were presented with a prominent Republican politician's inconsistent remarks, neuroscientists found that test subjects quickly exonerated their favorite politician through defensive reasoning. Moreover, this partisan thought process appears to be unconscious in that emotionally biased judgments helped the people in the experiment navigate away from the surprise of being wrong.[42] Other researchers who have studied such context collapse find that people have very real, jarring experiences when presented with unexpected information and social anecdotes on digital media.[43]

One important piece of the early scholarship on selective exposure may help us to understand how young people explore political content on social media. When communication scholars Steven Chaffee and Yuko Miyo interviewed 501 pairs of adolescents and their parents during the 1980 US presidential campaign, they confirmed that partisan predispositions motivated selective exposure that strengthened those predispositions.[44] However, the researchers were surprised to find that this tendency was strongest among adolescents. Chaffee and Miyo explain that "being comparatively new to politics, the adolescents respond more to the campaign, and they are considerably less likely than their parents to pay attention to the campaign communication of the candidate who is running in opposition to the one they favor."[45] It's plausible that this conclusion holds for young social media users as well.

Some of the best evidence about social media advertising and influence comes from the platforms themselves. A growing number of researchers work with social media data instead of polling data to answer basic research questions about public opinion dynamics.[46] Social media is important not only for obtaining news and political content but also as an indicator of public sentiment in elections and other political crises.[47] No matter the platform, social media users are producing a vast amount of data that is collected and analyzed to generate detailed psychological profiles of users that can provide insight into attitudes, preferences, and behaviors.

Indeed, the successful business model of these firms is to connect users algorithmically to content that is relevant to them individually, and target them with personalized advertising using systems in which political actors can "pay to play." The information users produce about themselves online helps craft the computational propaganda they are subsequently sent and the algorithmic allocation of peer influence—shaping voter preferences and turnout rates.[48] The study of the news consumption habits of social media users can also produce fine-grained analyses of the causes and consequences of political polarization.[49] Unfortunately, we don't really know how many people can tell junk news from real, but the social media platforms have created an entire industry to keep the distinction vague. They are immensely profitable and highly innovative at doing so.

Social media almost certainly facilitates selective exposure, mostly through *social* endorsements, peer effects, and repetition rather than through simply partisan frames and micro-targeting. On Facebook, friends share news from consistent ideological perspectives, rarely using diverse sources of political news and information. In a study by Eytan Bakshy and colleagues, Facebook users encountered roughly 15 percent less cross-cutting content in their news feeds due to algorithmic ranking, and they clicked through to 70 percent less of this cross-cutting content.[50] And psychologists have found that repeating things that are untrue—through a constant barrage of advertising and misinformation—can actually create the illusion of truth even in people who are knowledgeable.[51]

Within the domain of political news encountered on social media, selective exposure appears to drive attention. However, the underlying driver of attention is the social endorsement that is communicated through the act of sharing: social media users will not pay attention simply because a piece of political news is from a credible source or generated by a political party; they will pay attention because someone in their social network has signaled the importance of the content.[52] Other researchers have found that when the top search results about a political leader are positive, people say they will vote for that person. When they are shown negative results, people report that they are less likely to vote for that person.[53] So it should not be surprising that foreign governments seeking to interfere with domestic politics and shape public opinion inside a country would put resources into manipulating search results.

These businesses are about helping political actors find and mobilize a sympathetic public. They try to create the impression that there is public consensus on some topic or social problem when in fact there is none—the core component of what have come to be known as astroturf movements.[54]

What We Should Learn
from Junk News Operations

Why does junk news spread so effectively across social media? Governments have armies of staff and political parties have private consultants who produce large amounts of misinformation. We have explored how the algorithmic distribution systems of such social media as Facebook and Twitter ensure the directed delivery of content. And other research on human psychology demonstrates that many of us selectively expose ourselves to the content marketed by these junk news operations.

Our personal information habits and self-structured networks mean that the creative minds in Poland's Imitacja Consulting and Brazil's Imitação Services are guaranteed to have at least some receptive audiences in every country. But do these junk news operations actually have an impact? In the next chapter, we'll dive into one of the most significant contemporary examples of a social media misinformation campaign.

Of course, these firms operate in a media ecosystem that is eager to help circulate junk news. The relationship between such firms and corporate media is almost symbiotic, rather than adversarial, in that Poland's Imitacja Consulting and Brazil's Imitação Services stoke corporate media's appetite for sensational content that can draw in users. As digital culture scholar Whitney Phillips argues, corporate media needs viral digital content.[55] In politics and public life, the art of distributing junk news content involves a creative process of using data—and flare—to generate plausible-sounding content with politically outrageous implications.

These kinds of firms don't just operate in developing countries or young democracies. The pressure on major, mainstream news organizations to connect audiences and readers to revenue is global. Newsrooms from Scandinavia, Canada, Latin America, and India have experimented with attention-grabbing headlines, bot-generated content, and spicing the display of their own professionally produced news products with content from third-party providers.[56] Indeed, the pseudonyms for the firms studied here, Imitacja and Imitação, are the Polish and Brazilian words respectively for *imitation*—chosen both because they produce imitation news products and because every country has some similar kind of firm operating in its public life.

It is safe to say that every country in the world has some homegrown political consulting firm that specializes in marketing political misinformation. Their campaigns may be limited in scope, or they may be more about sowing confusion and negative campaigning than about pushing public opinion in one direction. Facebook admitted in the spring of 2019 that over a six-month period it removed three billion fake accounts and seven million hate-speech posts, and real US firms such as Devumi have managed fake accounts for high-profile actors and political figures.[57] To understand how the different components of lie machines—production, dissemination, and marketing—can fit together, let's next analyze the money trail and rhythms of one complete lie machine.

5

Tracing Impact and Influence

Myanmar used to be a country that inspired hope. The long-ruling military junta helped set up an election in 2010 and relinquished power to a civilian government the following year. Social media use soared as people in the country clamored to exercise newfound freedoms.[1] Facebook became the primary platform for public life and, in short order, an infrastructure for spreading hate speech and religious anger. A viral campaign against the Rohinga ethnic minority turned political rhetoric into violence and a complex humanitarian disaster.[2] Social media went from being the platform for community in a young democracy to a coordinating mechanism for genocide. Not only have tough regimes adopted social media, but they learn from each other. Myanmar's trolls got their training in Russia.[3]

The Russian government's spin machine also provides a good example of how big political lies get produced. The social media algorithms that Google, Facebook, Twitter—and even dating apps—use are examples of the computational systems that distribute big political lies. And firms such as Imitacja Consulting and Imitação Services illustrate how big political lies get marketed. When all the components of a lie machine work in harmony, the complete system of producing, distributing, and marketing political lies can have a significant impact on the course of current events, public understanding of crucial issues, and international affairs.

Social Media and Public Opinion

Lobbyists, political campaign managers, and politicians use social media to communicate directly with their constituents or the public at large. Tools like Twitter, Instagram, and Facebook allow campaigners to communicate without worrying about how journalists and editors may change, interpret, or fact-check the campaign messages. But editors and journalists provide a critical independent source of public knowledge and play an important role in evaluating the performance of elected leaders and public policy options. They check the claims of candidates who are running for election, and when political parties advertise, journalists do the fact-checking to investigate which political claims are most accurate. Removing professional editors and journalists from the flow of political news and information means that there are fewer checks on the quality of opinion and facts that circulate in public conversation.

But how do we know that communicating directly with voters—cutting professional news organizations out of the process—actually works? Social media firms themselves insist that fake news is only a tiny fraction of the content their users share and that they can't influence political outcomes.[4] (Though firms also insist to advertisers that ad campaigns purchased on their platforms have measurable influence!) Survey research estimates that the average US adult read and remembered at least one fake news article during the 2016 election period, with higher exposure to pro-Trump articles than pro-Clinton articles.[5] But the researchers found it tough to estimate the impact of the fake news articles they studied on voting patterns. Exposing voters to one additional television campaign ad raised vote share by 0.02 percent, according to one model, so if one fake news story had the same influence as one television ad, the overall impact of fake news on the vote would have been tiny.[6] Of course, these aggregated, national-level models for how modern lie machines work always miss the point of running a misinformation campaign on social media. Average effects across an entire country are not what modern lie machines are designed to create. It is network-specific effects, sited in particular electoral districts, among subpopulations, that are sought. The ideal outcome for political combatants is not a massive swing in the popular vote but small changes in sensitive neighborhoods, diminished trust in democracy and elections, voter suppression, and long-term political polarization.

Research finds that the good political ads really can motivate voters during a campaign. When political images are used to make emotional appeals and cue up enthusiasm, we respond by being motivated to participate and react with our existing loyalties. When such appeals are designed to stimulate fear, we can also be activated but are more likely to rely on in-the-moment thinking and be persuaded of new things.[7] Using social media also has a positive impact on a politician's share of the vote. Interestingly, the positive effect occurs when candidates for office push out lots of messages and broadcast their ideas. Interacting with voters on social media doesn't seem to drive up vote share.[8] Conversely, there is little consensus among researchers about the impact going negative has on voters. Some researchers argue that the impact is small, especially when staying positive can attract even more voters.[9]

Others argue that the effects of going negative can be especially potent for voters who are rarely engaged and not used to seeing political debate.[10]

Politicians always attack each other—obviously—and going negative, using manipulative rhetoric, or being aggressive in public debate doesn't have to involve propaganda and political lies. Moreover, most of the research on negative campaigning involves large samples of voters and exposure to broadcast media, and the effects of concentrated social network messaging will be greatly intensified for some voters and some communities. So the next important step in understanding the political economy of lie machines is to trace the complete process, from production to dissemination to marketing, and see how the money flows, how the political lies appeal, and how voters respond.

Political campaigns generally attract supporters by using as much personal data as possible to tailor and customize political messaging, whether those campaigns are chasing the support of constituents, voters, members, consumers, or any other group of people. Sometimes this data is used for what is called *political redlining*, which is itself a core process for managing citizens.[11]

Political redlining restricts our future supply of civic information by relying on assumptions about our demographics and present or past opinions. Redlining can occur in several ways. First, political consultants can delimit which population is less likely to vote and design a campaign strategy with only likely voters in mind. Second, redlining can occur when a campaign manager decides to filter political information—or pass along misinformation—to users who have signed up for specific content. Third, redlining can be self-induced when individual users privilege some information sources over others or set topical preferences that prevent their exposure to undesirable sources or topics. Political communication experts have long used the internet to sequester their supporters. From the point of view of campaign managers, political redlining is reasonable because politicians want to secure their base of supporters.[12]

Redlining allows political campaign managers to segment populations and perform a type of campaign triage. For example, if poor people from an ethnic minority rarely vote, or if they always vote for your opponent, it may not be worth spending time in their neighborhood trying to convince them to vote for you. If one city has consistently voted for one party for decades and there is no evidence that public sentiment is changing, why spend scarce campaign resources on advertising there?

Today's computational propaganda is built using the demographers' and statisticians' toolkit. Advances in measuring and modeling public opinion allow a political consultant to do more than simply identify and ignore nonvoters and committed opponents. Consultants can test the messages that might anger nonvoters enough to get them to vote or turn one of your opponent's voters into one of yours. A well-assembled lie machine builds in constant message testing, so that the most successful social media messages on one day get even wider distribution the next. This is why well-produced junk news can outperform real news in global circulation over social media.[13]

But can we demonstrate how lie machines work? Can we discover what metrics are used in constructing a mechanism for manipulating public opinion? It's probably impossible ever to model, without cooperation from Twitter, Facebook, or Google, how any particular post or search result changes a voter's thinking. The firms themselves can model these things. A few years ago, their staff and contract researchers showed off how they can influence their users in some academic articles.

But their poor ethical choices—coupled with the dramatic effects they revealed—attracted bad press, and their in-house researchers have since stopped writing about their findings.[14]

From outside the firms, researchers can set up highly controlled experiments to try and model the effects of junk news on voters, but the results of such research rarely reveal much about real-world settings. The outcomes would be so inorganic and unreal as to have little external validity because lab models would rarely extrapolate to real voters, real countries, or real elections. Instead, the gold standard in explanation in social settings is sensible causal narratives built through carefully organized evidence. As with any engine, taking the whole apart and reassembling the components helps us understand the mechanism. We will do just this to explain the impact and influence of one of the earliest, biggest lie machines to run in a democracy: the United Kingdom's Brexit campaign.

Mining Data for Political Inferences

Understanding how the modern political campaign works requires some knowledge of the data-mining industry, because this is the industry that supplies the information that campaign managers need to make strategic decisions about whom to target, where, when, with what message, and over which device and platform.[15] Most citizens do not know how much information about them is held, bought, and sold by campaigns, advertising firms, political consultants, and social media platforms. Sometimes political campaigns have clear sponsors and declare their interests, but on other occasions such disclosures are hidden. Sometimes the public can see what kinds of advertisements are produced and distributed during a campaign season, but at other times the advertising is discrete and directed and not archived anywhere. Sometimes campaigns de-

liberately spread misinformation, lies, and rumors about rivals and opponents.

Raw data is an industry term for information that has
not been processed or aggregated in some way. To make political inferences about someone, you usually need to take several kinds of data and put together an index that makes people
more comparable to one another. For example, you could label
someone a liberal if you acquire a list of their magazine purchases and find that they subscribe to a magazine where liberal commentators sometimes publish essays. But if you can
find more raw data and learn that they are registered with a
conservative party, that they have only ever voted for such a
party, and that all their friends also vote for conservative politicians, you can make more precise inferences that this person
should really be labeled a conservative. So the raw data about
many of our behaviors, such as magazine purchases, party
registration, voting history, and community ties, must be aggregated and weighed before reasonable political inferences
can be made. And the person in this example would probably
be scored as pretty conservative once all the relevant behaviors
were evaluated.

Credit card data often helps kick-start such labeling exercises. Even though the transactions are between a buyer and a
seller, credit card companies sell access to the transaction data
to many third parties, including advertisers, public relations
firms, and political consultants. Some third-party companies
pay for access to the raw data, which they then must analyze
themselves. Others prefer to pay for the finished analysis, so
they will hire consultants like the now-defunct Cambridge Analytica to process the data and report on the important trends.
The advantage of working with data brokers is that they can
merge data sets from multiple sources and make even more
powerful inferences.

Data mining has been an active industry for decades, so there are many kinds of aggregate categories available from data brokers.[16] The difference that social media makes is that these services provide new kinds of data that allow more detailed insight into how particular people think and feel.

For example, a traditional political consultant might have compiled data on voting history and magazine purchases and be able to provide a list of who in a district is liberal and who is conservative. Today, a consultant working with social media and device data will also be able to pull out data about the websites that individuals in the district have been visiting in the last week and merge that with existing demographic data from the district. If a small network of social media users has suddenly started trading links that betray a shift in political perspective or an openness to reconsidering their opinion on some issue, the consultant could work out what new message would encourage such thinking and advise a campaign on whom to send it to. If the consultant can tell the campaign what groups of people may be changing their opinions, highly targeted messages can be sent to those groups through social media. If the consultant can map these personal attributes onto a list of names, physical addresses, or social media profiles, very personal messages can be sent to named individuals.

It is extremely difficult to keep track of who is using either personal records or aggregated data about individuals. There are a few online services that convert the complex legal terms of service agreements that social media companies provide into more accessible language. For example, the website "Terms of Service; Didn't Read" will tell you how long social media services such as Facebook, Twitter, and YouTube hold on to data about your browsing history, or if they have no clear policy on that.[17] Terms of service agreements do not usually identify which specific third-party organizations are making use of your personal records.

Much of what we know about the qualities and quantities of both raw and aggregated data comes from the negative publicity around data breaches, court cases, and government inquiries. When a credit card company or consulting firm gets hacked and personally identifiable information is compromised, we can see the vast range of variables that are collected about people. For example, in October 2017, the large credit card company Equifax experienced a data breach that involved nearly 143 million customers in the United States and United Kingdom, and exposed email addresses, passwords, driving license numbers, phone numbers, and partial credit card details. In 2018, several massive hotel chains revealed that similar details on half a billion customers had been breached.[18] Political consultants are rarely caught working with hackers to steal data or interfere with the information infrastructure of another campaign. Usually they simply pay for voter intelligence from other firms that have legally bought access to raw and core data.

My own research into incidents of compromised records demonstrates that most so-called leakage is the result of corporate malfeasance.[19] Malicious hackers or foreign governments are not the ones who expose the most records. Rather, personal records are more likely to be compromised by dissatisfied employees or loose security guidelines. Typically, breach incidents involve organizational mismanagement: personally identifiable information accidentally placed online, missing equipment, lost backup files, and other administrative errors.

Sometimes people ask to see what data credit card companies or consulting firms keep on them. But companies usually share only the most obvious and least controversial variables and consider the rest to be their corporate intellectual property.

Consulting firms that work with political candidates, political parties, and lobbyists are reluctant to talk about what data they have and where they obtained it. Most people, most of the time, are shocked when they realize how much information such data brokers have. But because the data is politically sensitive, such firms tend to work with affinity groups where trust runs high. One consulting firm will develop a reputation for taking on liberal politicians and working on liberal issues, and another will gain a reputation for taking on conservative politicians and working on conservative issues. Because it takes significant work to merge data and make political inferences—this aggregated information becomes the intellectual property of the firm—most consulting firms will not reveal their information sources. They will usually tell clients only about big picture trends and aggregate findings, and they are unlikely to deliver any raw data.

In fact, both the firms that generate raw data and the consulting firms that aggregate it will stick to the letter of the law on privacy and data mining. By and large they interpret their obligations to customers very narrowly. If they can do some things with data in some jurisdictions but not others, it is common that they will strategically move data into the more permissive jurisdictions. If challenged by a customer, firms find it easier to rewrite a terms of service agreement and call an unethical practice a condition of service rather than consider some higher ethical or legal obligations to protect privacy or democracy.

Social Media at the Climax of the Brexit Campaign

Large numbers of voters in elections and referenda decide how they will vote in the final days of campaigns. One public opinion study of several years of voter decision making and voter psychology found that in every modern election, between 20 percent and 30 percent of voters either made up or changed their minds within a week of the vote. Half of those individuals did so on election day itself. This proportion can be higher in a referendum, where people tend to think that their vote is more significant. This appears to have been the case in the United Kingdom's 2016 referendum on leaving the European Union; one of the researchers' key findings was that 54 percent of respondents perceived the EU referendum as the most important vote in a generation, with 81 percent considering it to be among the top three.[20]

The Vote Leave campaign had an aggressive social media strategy that included not only spreading misinformation about the costs and benefits of EU membership but also overspending on its social media campaign. The misinformation strategy was identified during the campaign, but the overspending was not ruled illegal until months after the outcome had been decided. Fortunately, there are enough publicly available sources to present a picture of the campaign's strategy on producing, distributing, and marketing politically potent lies.

Three critical resources provide insight into how a lie machine such as the one run by Vote Leave can have an impact. The first is *All Out War: The Full Story of How Brexit Sank Britain's Political Class,* by the investigative journalist Tim Shipman. Though Shipman is not focused on analyzing the use of social media, his interviews of people with firsthand campaign knowledge reveal much about the digital strategy of Vote Leave. The second is a detailed account of Vote Leave's digital strategy by campaign director Dominic Cummings on his personal blog, https://dominiccummings.com. The third source is the UK House of Commons Digital Culture, Media and Sport Committee's investigative findings on disinformation and fake news after the referendum result. *Disinformation and "Fake News":* *Interim Report,* published in July 2018, contains information that Facebook furnished the committee concerning advertising on its platform by both Vote Leave and another group, BeLeave, during the campaign.

Like many national-level, high-stakes political campaigns in modern democracies, Vote Leave's digital strategy was ambitious and involved a global network of contractors and consultants. The campaign was largely conducted by the Canadian firm Aggregate IQ (AIQ). The firm began by building a "core audience" for Vote Leave's advertisements by first identifying the social media profiles of those who had already liked Eurosceptic pages on Facebook. Vote Leave advertised to this core audience to try and bring them onto its website, where they would be invited to add their personal details to its database. Another advertising tool within Facebook that AIQ used is called the Lookalike Audience Builder, which takes what is known about a group to help identify others for whom there might be some elective affinity.

This larger group, which AIQ designated the "persuadables," consisted of Facebook users with the same demographic features as the known, core audience of Eurosceptics. However, these persuadables had not previously expressed interest in Eurosceptic content on Facebook by "liking" Eurosceptic pages. This group of persuadables reportedly contained "a number of better-educated and better-off people." Cummings states in one of his blog posts that the persuadables were "a group of about 9 million people defined as: between 35–55, outside London and Scotland, excluding UKIP supporters and associated characteristics, and some other criteria."[21]

Vote Leave then began a process called *onboarding* in the industry, whereby sympathizers were turned into committed supporters of, donors to, and volunteers for the campaign. To do this, Vote Leave and AIQ deployed advertising targeting the persuadables and employed a three-step process. The first step was to invite the reader to click on an online advertisement, displayed on Facebook or other digital channels, so they could be taken to Vote Leave's website. Once the reader was there, the second step was to invite him or her to provide personal details—information that would also populate Vote Leave's database. The final step was to invite the reader to donate, share Vote Leave's messages, or volunteer for the campaign. Having social media users volunteer to communicate for the campaign was especially valuable because it generated additional organic growth in impressions without any cost to Vote Leave.

At each step in the onboarding process, the advertisements and messages were tested on an iterative basis. Ads or messages that failed to convince enough users to take the next step were reworked or changed entirely until a success threshold was reached. This threshold is known as the *conversion rate,* which I describe below. In his book, Shipman cites an anonymous source who described how Cummings evaluated each ad: "[He] approached each ad as if it were its own unique poll or focus group, and would compare those results to what they had observed from the data they had already been gathering. He was seeing what was being said in the polling and focus groups, and wanted to test those assumptions online to see that everything was in agreement with everything else. And when there were things which weren't, [Vote Leave would] exploit them or retool." Different ads were developed for the core and persuadable audiences. Core readers were served more demonstrative advertisements, whereas the persuadables reacted better to ads that appealed to their curiosity in weighing the arguments. "Is this a good idea?" and "Do you want to know more?" are cited by Shipman as typical messages.[22]

In May 2016, approximately four weeks before the referendum polling day, Vote Leave launched a competition to gather voters for its database. The competition promised a £50 million prize to anyone who could correctly predict the winner of all fifty-one games at Euro 2016, the soccer tournament. The purpose was to attract people who did not normally follow politics. Participants were asked to provide their name, mobile telephone number, address, and email details during the entry process. This data was fed into Vote Leave's database. More than 120,000 people entered the competition, and each of them received a reminder on June 23, 2016, to vote in the referendum.

Vote Leave also launched an app for smartphones. This app gamified the process of learning about Vote Leave's talking points, sending text messages to friends, watching Vote Leave's video material, and similar actions. On June 23, 2016, people reportedly sent seventy thousand messages via the app reminding their friends to vote.

Vote Leave's focus groups revealed how confused and fungible some voters were, changing their mind in response to whatever campaign ad they had seen most recently. So Dominic Cummings designed a "Waterloo Strategy" to deliver a huge barrage of Vote Leave advertisements to swing voters as close to the referendum as possible. An unidentified source from Vote Leave described the Waterloo Strategy: "Basically spend a shitload of money right at the end. We tested over 450 different types of Facebook ad to see which were most effective. We spent £1.5 million in the last week on Facebook ads, digital ads and videos. We knew exactly which ones were the most effective."[23]

In Shipman's account, Cummings is quoted as saying, "We ran loads and loads of experiments for months, but on relatively trivial amounts of money. And then we basically splurged all the money in the last four weeks and particularly the last ten days."[24] Most political campaigns expend the bulk of their resources in the final days of the campaign. But social media algorithms allow for the constant testing and refinement of campaign messages, so that the most advanced techniques of behavioral science can sharpen the message in time for those strategically crucial final days.

In his blog, Cummings writes, "One of the few reliable things we know about advertising amid the all-pervasive charlatanry is that, unsurprisingly, adverts are more effective the closer to the decision moment they hit the brain."[25]

The Vote Leave campaign decided to focus on consistent and simple political lies: first, that the United Kingdom was spending £350 million a week on the European Union, which it could spend instead on the National Health Service if it left the European Union; second, that Turkey, Macedonia, Montenegro, Serbia, and Albania were about to join the European Union; and third, that immigration could not be reduced unless the United Kingdom left the European Union. The £350 million claim was declared inaccurate by several experts, including Sir Andrew Dilnot, the chair of the UK Statistics Authority.[26] Similarly, the "Turkey claim" was untrue: there were no imminent plans for Turkey, Macedonia, Montenegro, Serbia, or Albania to join the European Union. So the first two were simply falsehoods—what we have since come to call "fake news." The third claim was simply a vague, controversial assertion: there is no evidence that countries must leave the European Union to affect their immigration rates. Nevertheless, Vote Leave pressed on with all these messages throughout the campaign, especially in the final days, and there were dozens of ads with such messages.[27]

Converting Voters through Digital Media

Every advertising campaign has what is called a *conversion rate*, and political campaigns are a form of advertising campaign. The conversion rate is the proportion of the audience that clicks on an online advertisement. Before social media existed, campaign managers simply bought banner ads, and they found that 1 percent of the people who see an ad will click on it, regardless of the topic. Of the people who do that in response to political messages, 10 percent will believe the message, and another 10 percent of those will be passionate enough about the topic to engage actively by buying the product, telling their friends about it, or participating in some other way.[28]

These days, campaign managers don't need to purchase and place banner ads because platforms like Facebook can serve up a purposefully selected sample of impressionable users. Because the social media firms can use their internal analytics to presort users, online political advertising goes directly to the people who are persuadable. Effectively, this compresses the process that involves a scattershot strategy of general banner ads. That is, Facebook users who see a political advertisement have already been preselected for being sympathetic, based on some prior analysis of data about them. Conservatively, we can estimate that 10 percent of those preselected users will click through to the website and believe the messages they read on the website to be true. A further 10 percent can then be expected to do something over and above believing the message: actively protesting, donating, or getting engaged in some other way.[29]

Shipman states in *All Out War* that Vote Leave was aiming for a 30 percent conversion rate from its advertisements and a 50 percent conversion rate from the messaging that the audience would receive on its website's landing pages. We don't know if they achieved these results, but constant A/B testing would help them achieve high conversion rates. That is, by randomly serving social media users two versions of an ad that differs only in one element—the choice of image or turn of phrase—ad designers can compare the conversion rates of each message. This gives a political communication expert even better information about how to refine and target future ads.

Shipman argues that Vote Leave was able to achieve these target conversion rates by regularly evaluating the advertisements' and political messaging's effects. If so, then Vote Leave was able to achieve an even higher conversion rate than 10 percent. This would mean that if, say, an ad had a reach of ten thousand people, Vote Leave could then expect three thousand viewers to click through the ad to arrive at its website, where it could expect fifteen hundred of those people to provide their personal data and get engaged with the campaign. However, the real conversion rate for Vote Leave's third step—getting someone to do something—is known only by Facebook and the other social media platforms where ads were placed. For the purpose of modeling the impact of directed political misinformation, let's proceed with the more conservative assumptions about what conversion rates may have been achieved.

It certainly helped that Vote Leave and BeLeave spent more than they were legally allowed. It is impossible to make a counterfactual judgement with certainty—spending the budget they were allowed might still have produced the same political outcome. Nevertheless, it is possible to estimate how many additional people the campaign reached, and converted, with the extra funding these campaigns used. And doing so reveals that the outcome of the referendum could have been affected, based on what we know about the Vote Leave campaign's impact and influence.

The UK Electoral Commission found in its report of July 17, 2018, that both Vote Leave and BeLeave breached campaign finance law: Vote Leave spent £449,079 in excess of the statutory limit, and BeLeave knowingly spent £666,016 more than the legal limit. The commission decided that both organizations had coordinated their campaigns and operated under a common plan of action, and fined both.[30] These spending offenses seem independent of each other because the funds came from different bank accounts. But it is very common for affinity campaigns with a shared agenda to develop the same spending and communications strategies. Effectively, the money used by both BeLeave and Vote Leave advanced the same campaign.

To determine whether these extra resources affected the referendum outcome, we need to compare Vote Leave's actual campaign with the campaign it would likely have run with the legal—but smaller—budget. Most of this excess spending would have gone to social media advertising. So, what kind of impact and influence might £449,079 in advertising have had, and could this have given Vote Leave the edge needed to win?

Illustrating the Brexit Campaign's Impact and Influence

One way to answer this is by illustrating how Vote Leave's campaign would have been affected if it had spent £449,079 less than it did. As I have said, Vote Leave put great emphasis on the last five days of the campaign, as part of the Waterloo Strategy. This strategy is detailed in Dominic Cummings's blog post of January 30, 2017, "On the Referendum #22: Some Basic Numbers for the Vote Leave Campaign," in which Cummings provides helpful charts.

The strategist reveals four digital advertising methods: video, search, display, and Facebook. Advertising on Facebook appears to be the largest part of the net spending. The campaign had a particularly successful run in its last few days of social media advertising. Facebook measures *impressions* to track the effectiveness of its advertising system. These are simply the total number of times an ad or post is displayed on a user's screen. In total, Vote Leave ads had 891 million Facebook impressions, with more than 30 million impressions per day in the last few days of the campaign. The campaign's video content was viewed by twenty-six million users—for at least ten seconds—with the highest viewing rates in the final days.

With such detailed information on how many people saw which kinds of advertising and how much that advertising cost, it is possible to model how much impact the excess campaign expenditures may have had on voters. In other words, Vote Leave spent £449,079 more than allowed by law, and we can estimate how many people the campaign reached with those resources. Since the charts report on the amounts paid in US dollars to US social media platforms, it makes sense to think this through in US dollars—at the time, this amount converted to $664,412.[31]

For a start, we could assume that these resources were all spent on all four types of digital advertising. This $664,412 would have covered the whole of Vote Leave's digital strategy for the last two days of the campaign, which the campaign said cost $525,000. Had they respected the spending rules, Vote Leave would have had to stop all its digital advertising sometime during the afternoon of Tuesday, June 21, 2016.

Because the vast majority of campaign spending was on Facebook advertising, it makes more sense to estimate how many days of Facebook campaigning this $664,412 would have bought. If Vote Leave had respected the referendum spending limits, the campaign would have had to give up ten days of Facebook advertising. Knowing how much the campaign was spending each day allows us to count backwards from voting day, June 23. The organization's spending in the last ten days adds up to just under the $664,412. If all other spending remained constant, forgoing $664,412 of Facebook spending would have meant that Vote Leave's Facebook ads would have ceased on Monday, June 13, 2016, ten days before the referendum vote.

Cummings stated in his blog that between June 7 and June 19 the campaign was achieving around 15 million impressions daily. These success rates rose over time, and over the last days the impressions topped 25 million, then 30 million, then 40 million, and ultimately 45 million, according to the campaign managers. Putting this together with Cummings's calculations, the excessive spending would have brought the campaign just under 24 million extra impressions each day for the final ten days of campaigning.

Conservative assumptions reveal that excess spending on social media advertising very likely resulted in 239 million extra impressions of Facebook ads (see table). If we take the low end of the campaign's stated conversion rates, then 30 percent, or almost 80 million impressions, would have been clicked on by real users whom Facebook recommended as persuadable. Of those, at least eight million people would very likely have been persuaded by the messaging, and around eight hundred thousand people would very likely have been energized enough to donate time or money to the campaign.

**Illustrative model of the impact of excessive
spending on social media advertising**

Date in June 2016	Days before voting	Excess Facebook spending	Excess impressions (million)	Excess user reach (million)
Tuesday, 14	10	$25,000	15	5
Wednesday, 15	9	$30,000	15	6
Thursday, 16	8	$10,000	15	10
Friday, 17	7	$50,000	15	6
Saturday, 18	6	$50,000	15	4
Sunday, 19	5	$75,000	15	5
Monday, 20	4	$75,000	28	8
Tuesday, 21	3	$110,000	32	10
Wednesday, 22	2	$125,000	42	12
Estimated totals		$650,000	239	80

Source: Author's calculations based on data available from multiple sources (Cummings, "On the Referendum #22").

Note: The campaign spent $664,412 more than allowed by law; for the purpose of being conservative and for ease of calculation, this is rounded down to $650,000 and distributed equally over the final 10 days. In total this probably yielded 239 million impressions, or roughly 24 million impressions per day. But these impressions would probably have been distributed unevenly, with higher daily rates on weekdays and at the climax of the campaign. At its peak, the campaign may have been converting half of its user impressions into supporters, but this illustrative model makes a more conservative assumption that one in three of these persuadable users would have been converted.

Vote Leave's social media advertisements would have reached millions of voters, but these ads were only one part of the overall leave campaign. Modern social media campaigning is often coordinated among affinity groups. Much of the overspending by Vote Leave was spent by BeLeave, which was equally effective. This is unsurprising given that BeLeave was also run by AIQ. Indeed, Vote Leave and BeLeave were *affinity campaigns,* meaning that their resources were spent with the same purpose. The Electoral Commission found, in its July 2018 report, that Vote Leave and BeLeave shared a common plan and that they both relied on AIQ's services. The commission reported:

> BeLeave's ability to procure services from Aggregate IQ only resulted from the actions of Vote Leave, in providing those donations and arranging a separate donor for BeLeave. While BeLeave may have contributed its own design style and input, the services provided by Aggregate IQ to BeLeave used Vote Leave messaging, at the behest of BeLeave's campaign director. It also appears to have had the benefit of Vote Leave data and/or data it obtained via online resources set up and provided to it by Vote Leave to target and distribute its campaign material. This is shown by evidence from Facebook that Aggregate IQ used identical target lists for Vote Leave and BeLeave ads, although the BeLeave ads were not run.[32]

The common messaging is evident in the choice of Facebook advertisements. BeLeave used some of the same kinds of misleading messages promoted by Vote Leave. For example, BeLeave wrote that "60 percent of our laws are made by from [sic] unelected foreign officials" (ad number 1430), and "We send £350m to the EU every week. Let's spend it on our priorities instead" (ad number 155).[33]

In other words, BeLeave replicated the big lies crafted by

the Vote Leave campaign, and in particular the £350 million claim. We can also model the impact BeLeave had using other kinds of data about that organization's portion of the campaign strategy. All in all, Vote Leave paid £675,315 to AIQ, through BeLeave, for their common strategic campaign.[34]

The data released by Facebook to the Electoral Commission shows that BeLeave embarked on a Facebook advertising campaign on June 15, 2016, a day after the first transfer of some of these excess financial resources. Copies of these ads are now public because Rebecca Stimson, UK head of public policy at Facebook, provided them to the House of Commons Digital Culture, Media and Sports Committee in response to a question.[35] In addition to providing the images and videos used in the advertisements themselves, Facebook revealed how well the different ads performed and broke down ad impressions by gender and region. This information not only allows for some modeling of the campaign but also reveals how some of Facebook's microtargeting options are used by campaign managers.

According to Facebook, BeLeave bought 120 advertisements and started running them on June 15, 2016—the day after Vote Leave and BeLeave paid AIQ for their campaign strategy. For the most part, once an ad started to run, it was not discontinued entirely. Of the 120 ads, only 2 ended their run before voting day. In the public information we have about this part of the campaign, the number of impressions each ad achieved—that is, the number of times it was displayed to Facebook users, regardless of whether they had already seen it or other advertisements from BeLeave—is given in ranges. Some ads garnered under a thousand impressions, whereas the successful ads produced five to ten million impressions.

By combining the lower and upper limits of the impression ranges for each ad, it is possible to arrive at an overall lower and upper limit for all the ads that ran. In total, BeLeave's ad campaign on Facebook resulted in between 47 and 105 million impressions.

In terms of reach, the Facebook records do not provide a total reach for each ad. The records do break down the reach for each ad group according to gender and age range, such as eighteen- to twenty-four-year-olds, as a percentage. For example, of one ad group's total reach, 10 percent went to females between the ages of twenty-five and thirty-four. Reach data is also provided by region and includes both views by targeted users and views by friends and family who received the ads because of sharing patterns within their network. The reach data suggests that, initially, BeLeave may have been targeting its ads at people between the ages of eighteen and forty-four, without any discernible gender bias. However, later groups of ads do not appear to show age bias. The audience for these ads was in England, and only a few Facebook users in Scotland, Wales, and Northern Ireland were targeted. In this way, Facebook's preselection process was consistent with what pollsters were saying about the limited appeal of Brexit to voters in those regions.

It appears from Facebook's spreadsheet that BeLeave's net return on its spending of £666,016 was not as successful as the other campaign, but it still reached millions of people. BeLeave garnered between 47 and 105 million impressions over eight days. Following the same conservative assumptions about conversion used above, we can estimate that between 4.7 and 10.5 million voters would have seen these ads and been persuaded, and between 470,000 and 1 million voters would have been energized enough to donate money or time to the campaign. Importantly, Northern Ireland's Democratic Unionist

Party and a group called Veterans for Britain were other affinity campaigns contributing to these ad networks in various ways.

Working on the other side of this referendum question was the Remain campaign, which spent its resources in a legal way and ended its digital advertisements on the day before voting. Campaign managers normally try to control spending to save resources for the final push. This would be consistent with best practices in political campaigning: you keep track of your legally allowed campaign budgets and time the purchase of ads so that the climax in ad spending coincides with the climax of the campaign period—right to the final hours—in which you are legally allowed to campaign.

In the final days before voting, the Vote Leave campaign's political redlining of UK voters would have been most effective. Recall that between 20 percent and 30 percent of voters make up or change their minds within a week of the vote and that half of those individuals do so on election day itself. Vote Leave's campaign engineer Dominic Cummings noted that "something odd happened on the last day, spending reduced but impressions rose by many millions so our cost per impression fell to a third of the cost on 22/6 which is not what one would expect and we never bothered going back to Facebook to ask what happened."[36] The early end to Remain's advertising had two consequences. On the last day of voting, only the Brexit campaign's messages would have been going out to the 10 to 15 percent of voters who had not decided how to vote. Simultaneously, the lack of competition would have caused the cost of each advertisement to drop. Facebook's advertising prices are determined through an automated auctioning system, and prices are based on the competition between advertisers seeking the same or overlapping audiences. With the Remain campaign no longer bidding, the Brexit campaign's illegal ad budgets would have gone much further in those final hours.

From Campaign Spending to Political Outcomes

Measuring the impact of how political information is presented over social media is tough. The social media firms don't admit much about how they can affect people when it comes to political opinion, though they certainly claim much about how they can affect people when it comes to consumer behavior. In one small study of voter turnout run by Facebook itself on its own users, one single tweak in platform design caused 340,000 more voters to vote on election day.[37]

It is important to remember that rich data on voters doesn't just feed the complex learning algorithms of the social media firms. An important part of the mechanism is offline, and such data feeds the apps that advise campaign workers on whom to visit during the campaign period and with what message. Both Brexit and Trump campaign canvassers used apps that could identify the political views and personality types of a home's inhabitants, allowing canvassers to ring only at the doors of houses that the app rated as receptive. Canvassers had scripts tailored to the personality types of residents and could feed reactions back into the app; that data then flowed back to campaign managers to refine overall strategy.[38]

In the end, the result of the 2016 EU referendum in the United Kingdom was that 48 percent of voters preferred to remain and 52 percent of voters preferred to leave. The Brexit campaign won by just over 1.2 million votes. A swing of about 600,000 people would have been enough to secure victory for Remain. Almost 80 million extra Facebook ads would have been served up to persuadable UK voters during the period of excess spending. The Brexit campaign machine was aiming for a conversation rate of 50 percent. But even taking the more conservative industry conversion rate of 10 percent, at least 8 million people would not only have accepted the messaging but clicked through to Brexit campaign content in that sensitive moment. More than 800,000 of those Facebook users would have accepted and consumed the content, which included several lies, but also would have been energized enough to engage more deeply with campaign activities. It is very likely that the misinformation campaign reached millions of voters throughout the campaign period and that the excessive spending helped secure a political outcome in the referendum result.

I have made some conservative assumptions about measuring the effects. First, these Brexit communication campaigns were targeting likely voters and, in the final days, were running after the Remain campaign had reached the statutory spending cap and stopped advertising. Second, this conclusion is based on Vote Leave data alone—better data from the other affinity campaigns would allow for a more refined estimate of the overall impact. Still, we can conservatively say that Vote Leave and BeLeave would have reached tens of millions of people over the final days of the campaign, only because they spent more than legally allowed on a savvy digital advertising strategy. Third, Vote Leave's dynamic, iterative ad-testing system would have achieved rising success rates over time. In this breakdown I have worked with a conservative 10 percent conversion rate rather than the 50 percent rate that campaign managers aspired to and may have, on occasion, achieved. Fourth, these findings are based only on Facebook advertising data. The supplementary video, search, and display strategies would have reached additional voters and hit the persuadable voters many times over. Last, the cost of Facebook advertising decreased on the day of the referendum itself, meaning that Vote

Leave's excess spending would have afforded even more impressions than estimated in this conservative model. Much of what political communication scholars know about voter influence is generated from models of how US voters learn. So it is possible that UK voters would have had different conversion rates. Since both countries are English-speaking, advanced democracies with similar media environments, the comparison is probably safe.

While these simple calculations illustrate how a social media campaign was organized to influence voters, many other factors could have affected the outcome. But with the available evidence on the spending and strategy of these campaigns, we can reconstruct the influence models that campaign managers themselves use to shape political outcomes. Moreover, this evidence allows us to illustrate how the many components of a complex lie machine—systems of production, distribution, and marketing, especially misinformation and social media algorithms—can together make an impression on millions of voters.

Many kinds of politically motivated lies are easy to catch under scrutiny, but it isn't always possible to get people to stop believing them. For philosophers, a lie involves telling people something you believe to be false with the intention that they believe what you say. Unfortunately, this understanding of what a lie is fails to capture many significant forms of deceptive behavior that we now see in complex political misinformation campaigns. The Brexit campaign used misleading images as well as words in messages that sowed doubt and confusion. And platforms such as Facebook may not care what its users believe so long as the false stories generate advertising revenue. Lie machines are a significant threat to democracy because they give us the wrong information, or poor-quality information, that prevents us from making informed decisions on policy issues or on election day. Fortunately, we've deconstructed and dismantled the complex mechanism of producing, distributing, and marketing big political lies, so in the next chapter we'll explore the best options for protecting democratic institutions. How do we save democracy?

6

Future-Proof Solutions for a Data-Rich Democracy

L ie machines have a purpose.[1] They deliberately misrepresent symbols. They appeal to emotions and prejudices and use our cognitive biases to bypass rational thought. They repeat big political lies to misinform some people and introduce doubt among even the most active and knowledgeable citizens. They work because we ourselves generate the data used to craft manipulative content. Lie machines have been constructed in many kinds of countries: authoritarian governments build them to sustain their power; in democracies, political parties, lobbyists, and candidates for elected office build them in the pursuit of power. But they are all made up of the same core components: political actors producing the lies, social media firms doing the distribution, and paid consultants doing the marketing.

Disinformation campaigns will continue to be launched against voters in democracies. For every new social media platform, every new design idea on every platform, and every new digital device, someone will work to integrate the innovation into a computational propaganda campaign. Over the next few years, every new device added to a network will generate data that will be valuable for some kind of political inference.

Many factors have caused junk news to spread so rapidly, with diverse effects in different countries. Journalism, especially print media, has been transformed since the arrival of online media and platforms such as Google and Facebook. The most professional news outlets in every country now must compete with content producers—domestic and international—who produce junk news that is sensational, conspiratorial, extremist, and inflammatory commentary packaged as news. Changes in online ad markets and the mechanics of ad placement have encouraged the growth of junk news by making it profitable for websites to make use of political clickbait ads.

Technology firms have reacted, albeit slowly. In democracies, there have been major government investigations, criminal inquiries, and several years of bad press. Platform initiatives range in scope and seriousness—and vary from country to country depending on the importance of the advertising market. In advanced Western democracies with a significant user base and a major language group, the firms have had to show initiative in the face of political attention. In emerging democracies elsewhere in the world, the platforms haven't crafted special responses and have often ignored local demands for accountability.[2]

For now, it is unclear what makes some countries more vulnerable to junk news than others. Europe, Canada, and Australia may be more immune than the United States because levels of education are higher and public broadcasters create a professional culture for journalism and help maintain high standards of journalism. Having a diverse range of news producers is probably important for public life. Credible public agencies and independent researchers that have good communication strategies can also improve the flow of high-quality information. Huge amounts of information about our behavior, attitudes, and aspirations have been collected by businesses that profit from our cognitive biases.

Most people who read a tweet or a Facebook post don't click on the links that provide evidence. They see the cover message that comes from someone in their network and assume that the link backs up what's said in the tweet. If the people behind the junk news campaign can include a link to a story from a major news brand, they will. And it takes a close read to see that the content of the tweet isn't backed up by the story. Sometimes the evidence in the news story supports the opposite of what the misleading tweet says.

Russia and China are certainly superpowers when it comes to launching campaigns of misinformation, but we can expect other regimes to develop their capacity to influence global public opinion. Turkey, Iran, and Venezuela are already exercising their lie machines on key human rights issues and international affairs. Authoritarian governments tend to learn from each other, and we have seen more and more such regimes applying these techniques. In 2017, there were twenty-eight countries with formal organizations—secret government agencies, lobbyists, political parties, and candidate campaigns—using social media algorithms to distribute misinformation. The number rose to forty-eight when the same inventory was taken only a year later. In 2019, we found seventy. As more and more political actors realize that they may be targeted by others, the number of foreign governments and political actors pumping resources into producing lie machines will only grow.

We may also notice an increasing number of political

parties, foreign powers, and industry lobbyists developing disinformation campaigns for single issues and legislative campaigns, not just elections. Although many of the campaigns studied here occurred during elections, the campaigns were usually about polarizing issues, not about candidates for office. And many divisive issues, such as abortion, gun control, and immigration, regularly surface between elections. Perhaps more fundamentally, the coterie of communications advisers, social media gurus, and political campaign managers who make their consulting services available between elections have proven their worth during elections.

And as foreign powers grow increasingly adept at crafting messages and segmenting populations for influence, persuadable voters and minority communities will remain targets. Given the disinformation campaigns that have been—and currently are—targeting voters in the United States, for example, I would guess that foreign actors will continue to aim future disinformation campaigns at African American voters, Muslim American voters, white supremacist voters, and voters in Texas and other southern states. Across the world's democracies I expect that the strategy will remain the same: push disinformation about public issues, discredit politicians and experts, and prevent particular types of voters from participating on election day. In authoritarian regimes, especially those that have rigged elections, ruling elites will continue to use these strategies on their own citizens. In many kinds of countries, political lies are a big business.

The Political Economy of Big Lies

Lie machines will certainly evolve in the coming years. They will produce more varied forms of content, from fake fact-checking news sites to fake videos and fake statistical data sets.

In this book I've traced the global chains of creation and consumption for junk news—who produces it and conveys it, and where it goes. The motivations for building lie machines are likely to remain constant: they are built either to make money or to promote ideology, and they are most powerful when both motivations are in play. Tracing this detailed process exposes the global political economy of big lies but also reveals what makes some democracies more resistant and resilient than others to the phenomenon.

Lie machines are created by social media firms and political communication consultants, fueled by shady politicians and lobbyists, and subject to market forces. Propaganda is not new, but the complex global mechanism of social media algorithms—the massive distribution, combined with sophisticated targeting—is new. Obviously, we can't combat political lies if we don't understand how they are made. It is my hope that understanding the mechanism of a lie machine can help us mitigate the impact of computational propaganda in the years ahead.

From Russia to Brazil and from the United States to India, I've taken you through the various business models for producing lies for profit. The markets for misinformation are largely unregulated, but it is not clear that social media firms—or politicians—want to do much about the problem. The tech giants compete for advertising revenues and design ever more computationally sophisticated ways of bringing advertising to more people. Political campaign managers, foreign agents, and savvy lobbyists will continue to exploit the same advertising mechanisms that help the Kardashians market themselves and their lifestyle products. Lie machines have flourished on social media such that we are past the point of industry self-regulation. Ultimately the solution must involve public policy oversight and some market-shaping initiatives.

Half a century of research reveals that, overall, most media effects are minimal and vague.[3] We rarely find moments when large numbers of people have rapidly and wildly changed their opinion because of a political campaign. Most media technologies—social media included—have effects at the margins of society and among small numbers of voters. But as we have now seen, those margins can be important. A percentage point change in how a politician is perceived can end a career and alter the tone of an otherwise civil conversation. In politically competitive swing districts, where people are evenly split on whom to elect or which policy to implement, a misinformation campaign can provide the 1 or 2 percentage points to make a vote change from 50–50 to 51–49. Large amounts of misinformation about an issue can prevent consensus, create political deadlock, and have serious consequences for the health and welfare of communities and neighborhoods.

The problem isn't that a fraction of the entire public is the target audience for misinformation. It is that a fraction of the public in particular towns, provinces, states, and electoral districts is the target. Lie machines can't reach and confuse everybody. But they can radically mislead small numbers of us, confirming biases and activating citizens for the wrong reasons. And they can subtly guide large numbers of us to distrust the institutions of democracy.

The key parts of a modern lie machine are political figures who craft lies, social media platforms that distribute the lies, and the consultants who profit by selling the lie to you. Altogether, these three components make an instrument that can produce a rich variety of political lies—simple or complex— in the form of computational propaganda. As I've shown, computational propaganda is often used to attack civic society. The "computational" part of the equation is an important one.

Data-driven tools such as bots and social media algorithms allow small groups of actors to direct subversive content and false information at persuadable users. Rapid cycles of sharing, repurposing, and further dissemination by the lie machine quickly erode public understanding.

The absence of human editors in our news feeds also makes it easy for political actors to manipulate social networks. We've found political leaders in many young democracies actively using automation to spread misinformation and junk news. It seems that social media has gone from being the natural infrastructure for sharing collective grievances and coordinating civic engagement to becoming a computational tool for social control that is manipulated by crafty political consultants and unapologetic dictators.[4]

The bots I analyzed earlier are designed to behave like real people, for example by automatically generating and responding to conversations online. They amplify or suppress political messages and are activated and deactivated at will by political paymasters. Savvy users may be able to spot them manually, but even engineers at social media firms sometimes struggle to identify them operating in real time. And it takes enormous amounts of independent research, media attention, and public outrage to force the leadership of social media firms to respond.

The manipulation of public opinion over social media platforms has emerged as a critical threat to public life. Around the world, a range of government agencies and political parties are exploiting social media platforms to spread junk news and disinformation, exercise censorship and control, and undermine trust in the media, public institutions, and science. At a time when news consumption is increasingly digital, artificial intelligence, big data analytics, and black-box algorithms are being leveraged to challenge truth and trust—the very corner-stones of our democratic society.

Social media manipulation is big business. Since 2010, political parties and governments have spent more than half a billion dollars on the research, development, and implementation of psychological operations and public opinion manipulation over social media. In a few countries, this includes efforts to counter extremism, but in most countries, this involves the spread of junk news and misinformation during elections, military crises, and complex humanitarian disasters. In an important way, the business incentives to develop AI for political purposes are firmly in place.

It is always difficult to predict how a sociotechnical system will evolve, but we should be confident that this one will. What will new technologies, such as machine learning and other AI tools, mean for political communication in the years ahead?

Scenarios for AI-Generated Propaganda

Political actors and profiteering firms use social media algorithms and big data to manipulate public life. What will happen when the machine learning systems that analyze our behavior, attitudes, and aspirations become sophisticated enough to operate with a degree of autonomy? We already have sophisticated bots engaging people in political conversation and machine learning algorithms sending us ideologically loaded content. Will AI be tasked with political persuasion?

The prospect of AI-generated propaganda is serious. AI-enabled propaganda will make use of privately held databases about personal behaviors, attitudes, and aspirations, the content we generate, and the algorithms of social media firms to manipulate public opinion across a diverse range of platforms and device networks, device data, collected through the internet of things, will also help refine political inferences.

One safe bet is that AI will be used for political redlining. Machine learning is good at studying behavioral patterns we don't even know we have. It looks for correlations among thousands, if not millions, of variables, learning from matrices of information that are bigger than a human can conceive of. Advertisers can already predict a person's mood months in advance, and employers can already use machine learning to evaluate which potential employees will get pregnant within a year or who will have depression and anxiety at work.[5] Machine learning, with similar data, will certainly reveal who can be invigorated to vote and participate in politics and who can be discouraged from voting on election day.

More and more political parties, government agencies, and data-mining firms are playing with machine learning tools, and such tools will be very useful for helping to manage public life where independent journalism is marginalized, roped to a ruling regime, or just deficient. At the moment, many of us can spot the unsophisticated chatbots that might be talking at us. But the best bots have been successful at poisoning many kinds of political conversations. AI-driven fake users will be even more convincing because they will be trained to be dynamic and interactive—just like our human friends and family.

So the question is not whether political parties in democracies will start using AI on one another—and us—but when.[6] AI-driven fake citizens or campaign staff could be unleashed at a strategic moment in a campaign cycle or by a lobbyist targeting key districts at a sensitive time for an important piece of legislation. The least sophisticated bots have had immense roles in political discourse. So AI-driven fake citizens might influence popular opinion in similar ways. Real-time interactions with AI-backed user accounts are going to be harder and harder to see through. With an industry of political consultants eager to have the most AI-enabled automata at election time, voters may just have to get used to the possibility that their interactions with a political candidate or party will be mediated by AI. But for now, with most internet users barely able to manage their cookies, the possibility that AI will have significant power to interfere with public opinion during politically sensitive moments is very real.

Artificial intelligence will have a role in political life in all types of regimes in the years ahead. In democracies, it will probably be used to charm and provoke voters, spread misinformation, and take advantage of rich personal data to make powerful emotional appeals. For countries that hold elections, AI-driven fake users will become a new, serious, and internal threat to their democracy. In the United States, political campaigning is an aggressive, big-money game, where even candidates in local and precinct races may think that some AI-enabled campaign techniques would be a cost-effective campaign strategy. In authoritarian regimes, it will have a role in social control, policing, and preventing or managing political conversations in ways that benefit ruling elites.

Social media is the conduit for modern political culture and conflict. Almost everyone is present and accounted for on social media platforms. We may appear through the user accounts we have deliberately created on the platforms. But firms also build models of those of us who are not users, by creating a digital shadow of us with data collected from other sources.[7]

With the ability to have multiple simultaneous political conversations, political AI will devour large volumes of data, consume lots of bandwidth, and engage many people at once. But the more pernicious problem concerning trust in politics is that AI-enabled social media accounts will be even better than today's chatbots at passing as real people in our own so-cial networks. It is already hard for us to protect our own on-line identities. Having to verify everyone else's will diminish public trust in the value of political debate or we'll have to sur-render to the notion that AI will be engaging us in political conversation. Political conversations, however, don't need fur-ther subterfuge.

AI Apps We Don't Want

Artificial intelligences are collections of algorithms and data that simulate learning, reasoning, and classification—all tech-niques of use in the production, distribution, and marketing of political lies. AI would be able to take advantage of the stores of data about us to construct more engaging fake users who don't simply respond with scripted commentary. They would respond more organically and have the appearance, social cues, and individual habits that would play on our empathy. These fully automated political actors would work to bolster particu-lar politicians and policy positions—supporting them actively and enthusiastically while simultaneously drowning out dis-senting voices. They would be less reliant on human troll armies to manufacture consensus around a political idea or policy and better able to generate attractive appeals to encourage us to join a social movement. In fact, we can use our experience with the early modes of automated and algorithmic lie ma-chines to extrapolate how AI will likely be used in political life in the years ahead.

First, if the trends continue unabated, AI will be used to polarize voters on issues. As I've demonstrated, known Rus-sian social media accounts simultaneously promoted political action by groups likely to come into conflict with each other. This strategy involved pitting United Muslims of America against the Army of Jesus in public arguments. It drew in African American political activities around Black Lives Matter to protest police shootings and encouraged civil strife with a Blue Lives Matter movement made up of citizens expressing solidarity with police.

One campaign encouraged Muslims and Christians to convert their spiritual commitments into action in a competitive political arena. The other encouraged people upset with police shootings of young black men to confront—online and face to face—groups that support the police. The goal has been to get groups of voters to confront each other angrily over social media and in the streets. Similarly, video content, edited and taken out of context, makes immigrants seem a threat to veterans or tells one community that the police need their support while telling another that the police are abusing them. If AI systems are applied in public life by some producers of big political lies, we can reasonably expect them to radicalize and polarize our perspectives on faith-based issues, social inequality, and the threat of immigrants.

Second, if patterns remain the same, AI will be used to promote or discredit politicians, presidential candidates, and other public figures. Foreign-backed rumor mongering is not new, but it is much more strategically targeted within districts and by voter demographics than before. It is already safe to say that every public figure on the national stage is either attacked by or benefits from highly automated or fake social media accounts, and whether these campaigns are managed by foreign governments depends on the issues involved and the time of the campaign season. If political campaign managers have the financial resources to keep an AI advocate running all day long, actively engaging citizens with the genuine enthusiasm, empathy, and intelligence of a neighbor or friend, that's better than any volunteer!

Third, if the application of AI to politicking is like what we've seen so far, AI-driven political campaigns will be used to discourage citizens from voting. Voter suppression is a common messaging strategy aimed at voters who might support a candidate that a foreign government finds unpalatable. For example, voters are often told that voting day has been postponed or that they can text message their vote in or that their polling station has moved. If a political campaign, government, or lobbyist can use sophisticated AI to identify who won't be voting their way and why, it will be easier to target those voters with messages that either carry misinformation about the logistics of voting or erode voters' trust in the belief that their vote will have an impact.

It is difficult to know how many people in the world's democracies have seen basic forms of such messages or how many voters were influenced by them. Only the social media firms themselves could share that data or estimate those probabilities accurately. But in most countries around the world, it is safe to assume that social media platforms have efficiently delivered such messages and advertisements to voters and that these messages had an influence, in different ways, in different states, and in conjunction with all the other variables that can shape public understanding of issues and the outcomes of elections.

Finally, we have probably learned enough from the diffusion of current misinformation tools to say that AI-generated political propaganda will have a global and multiplatform reach. An array of regimes and political parties manipulate public opinion over social media. Around the world, a range of government agencies and political parties are exploiting social media platforms to spread junk news and disinformation, exercise censorship and control, and undermine trust in the media, public institutions, and science.

Sophisticated machine learning systems would certainly allow these agencies and parties to do more of the same over several platforms at once. AI would allow the agile manipulation of larger and larger—and therefore more complex—digital artifacts. At the moment, machine learning can generate specific text and target ad content at particular voters. But large video files of fake events, complete archives of fake data, and organic-looking, cross-platform content production would become easier to produce through machine learning. Much innovation originates in countries where political parties are spreading disinformation during elections. In countries where government agencies feel threatened by junk news and foreign interference, they respond by developing their own computational propaganda campaigns to answer their enemies. Lie machines are beginning to involve encrypted chat platforms that are designed for discrete communication between individuals and small groups and are not public in the same way that Facebook and Twitter are. Sophisticated machine learning might allow for the creation of digital personalities that can spoof the intimate interaction possible on an encrypted chat platform such as WhatsApp, Telegram, or WeChat.

The structure of our political communication will evolve as our information technology develops.[8] Most of us experience the internet directly through our computer browser or mobile phone, but increasingly the internet is made up of connected devices like modern refrigerators and lightbulbs. Industry analysts estimate that connected consumer goods and industrial equipment will amount to seventy-five billion devices by 2025.[9] Only a fraction of these, a few billion at most, will be personal computers, tablets, and smartphones. In the next five years, more than a thousand networked nanosats— relatively small, low-power satellites that operate in formation—

will be launched into space. Drone production, whether for the military or hobbyists, is difficult to track. But government security services have them, and activists and humanitarian organizations do, too. An OECD report on the internet of things estimates that whereas a family of four has a handful of connected devices today, that same family will have fifty connected devices by 2022. Each will have sensors and a radio that can broadcast information about the time, the device's location, its status, and how it has been used.[10]

Currently, lie machines are built from social media algorithms and junk news content, but the internet of things, artificial intelligence, and augmented and virtual reality are the next technologies that have great potential to change the way citizens explore political news and content and interact with one another. As a growing number of consumer products come chipped, with embedded power supplies, small sensors, and an internet address, more and more of our behavior will be recorded by the manufacturers of those products. As AI tools get better at analyzing this behavioral data, the sophistication of political inferences about what we want and what we will respond to will grow significantly. As augmented and virtual reality technologies allow both subtle and overt images to be placed directly in our field of vision, advertisers will have more opportunities to place this sophisticated content in front of us. Given what we now know about the evolution of lie machines, it is not so hard to imagine how the production, distribution, and marketing of political lies may evolve in the years ahead into truly enormous mechanisms for social control.

The real threats to democracy lie ahead of us. So far, we haven't seen true artificial intelligence and device data applied to the production of political messages. But that is coming, and machine learning algorithms will soon be working with the vast amounts of behavioral data collected through the internet of things as well as through social media. Each time a government runs a successful disinformation campaign in another country, other governments learn from it. As political leaders who successfully integrate automation and social media algorithms into their campaign strategies get elected, new political challengers will want to do that, too.

What's next? Unfortunately, the lie machines we have exposed are just early forms of automation that have filled our inboxes and social media feeds with junk. Machine learning political chatbots are now in development, and these are slightly more sophisticated and interactive scripts for talking politics. Are you sure that we evolved from primates? There's a chatbot that will make you reconsider this. Is climate change real? Should we inoculate our kids? Chatbots have become the hot tool for industry lobbyists seeking to promote junk science. And the next step is to put artificial intelligence algorithms behind these bots.

We can also expect foreign governments to apply these techniques and develop these messages for multiple platforms. They will move to whichever social media platform has voters and citizens. The earliest of these misinformation campaigns began on Twitter and were then used on Facebook in the run-up to the 2016 US presidential election. More recently, they have moved to Instagram, where they can find more young voters, and to social media platforms that are even more supportive of sensational, conspiratorial, extremist political conversations, such as Gab.

Advances in artificial intelligence and machine learning may also find quick political application—technology in the service of power. Currently, influence operations from foreign governments, shady politicians, and industry lobbyists take advantage of the algorithms built by social media firms and search engines to customize the delivery of disinformation. AI, machine learning, and natural language processing will be used not only for individual targeting but also for individually customized content. Videos and text can be crafted using knowledge of credit card purchases or device data from our mobile phone or our internet-connected refrigerator. The global market for such data—legal and otherwise—is thriving, and it has agglomerated large caches of privately held data. Even with swift government action to shut down trade in personal data, analysts would have sufficient data to train machine learning algorithms to have sophisticated political conversations with many voters, particularly those in wealthy countries where electronic transactions have long been part of social life.

If the history of technology in politics provides any lessons, then it is safe to say that someone will use AI to make political inferences from such behavioral data. Vast swaths of fresh data will make political targeting even more authoritative. This rich data will also likely be used to train AI to advise political campaign managers on strategy and actively converse with citizens.

With the current trend line, it would take a concerted effort by social media platforms to rework the global political economy of junk news and ensure that AI and machine learning tools are *not* applied for political gain. Indeed, restoring some sensible structure to how we deliberate is beyond the remit and capability of any one firm or any one public agency.

How to Break Lie Machines

Understanding how lie machines produce, distribute, and market junk news has meant breaking them down into their component parts, and we may even be able to break many of them for good. Junk news is just the symptom of the problem, however. It is merely the indication or presentation of a disorder. The disorder is the monopolization of information about public life by a few technology firms.

For many centuries churches kept the best records of public life, such as information about births and deaths, basic demographics, and who was paying taxes. Then, for several centuries, governments and libraries held the best records of public life. Now a handful of technology firms have the best data on us as individuals, on our networks, and on public life. They develop tools for exploiting those networks for their advertisers. They aggressively take advantage of our psychological predilection for selective exposure and elective affinity.

The manipulation of public opinion over social media platforms has emerged as a critical threat to public life. The solution to this problem necessarily involves research and public policy oversight. Technology firms occasionally share small amounts of data, but providing a regular flow of data about public life to elections administrators, researchers, and civil society groups is the best way to give democracy a chance to recover.

If these trends in data generation and social media use continue unchecked, this thing we think of as "the public" will almost fully dissolve. There will be fewer and fewer widely shared norms and moments of common purpose, and less collective empathy. The impact of junk news, junk science, and ideas about junk policy will be felt through more angry and unproductive political conversations, deadlock in our decision-making institutions, and intractable public policy problems. Misinformed voters will elect more politicians who play up to the fears expressed in junk news. Misinformed political leaders will choose to go with their gut rather than listen to scientific advisers, policy experts, or voters. It has proven too hard to make sense of the glut of information available, and critical thinking has become a generalized skepticism that everything is suspicious. And if everything is suspicious, as Mark Andrejevic observes, we default to drawing courage from our own prejudices and preconceptions.[11] If this remains unchecked, science itself will have an irregular, ad hoc role in public life—becoming a rhetorical tool for use in every campaign that claims to have exposed long-hidden truths. To keep our communities and countries healthy and functional, we need to stop building lie machines, and break down the existing ones.

The problem is that most social and political opinion data is currently held and manipulated by private firms. These firms buy, sell, and steal personal data as a service to lobbyists, foreign governments, disreputable politicians, and individual crackpots who want to promote misinformation. Social media is not designed to help us deliberate, but new advertising and data management guidelines could make this possible. This argument is well made by Siva Vaidhyanathan in his book *Antisocial Media: How Facebook Disconnects Us and Undermines Democracy*, but it is important to remember that the cause of deception in politics is both the algorithms that have been designed by social media engineers and the content that has been produced by underhanded politicians, lobbyists, and political communications consultants. After all, lie machines are a complex sociotechnical system.

Social media needs to be designed to highlight emerging consensus rather than heated conflict. Right now, most content promotion systems bring squabbles to the fore. The platforms solicit us to contribute to disagreement and argument. Rather than revealing the timeline of an evolving conversation, the platforms highlight quarrels and conflict. Machine learning, however, could also help reconcile differences, identify common ground, and draw in new users to see how consensus strengthens or dissolves.

Social media platforms have transformed the global economy of propaganda production. Previously, large governments generated massive propaganda campaigns, while lobbyists and advertisers tested the limits of regulators with negative campaigning, false advertising, and rhetorical strategies. Our new political world isn't that simple. Citizens are inundated with computational propaganda from many players, including foreign governments. Social media firms effectively privatized propaganda production. Individuals targeted in a campaign receive much more frequent, personalized appeals. And the content comes over our own trusted networks of family and friends, over digital technologies, social media platforms, and device networks that by default we tend to trust more than other media. None of us have been trained to think critically about the persuasive messages that come from our own social networks. And social media platforms have been designed to promote excitement and polarizing content, not civility and consensus. Modern citizens need to upskill; platforms need a redesign.

Our new political world is defined by unique configurations of control over how we express our political attitudes and aspirations. With the shadow of data we cast as we move through our daily lives, we inadvertently reveal our preferences more regularly than citizens of the past. Our credit card purchases and city travels generate data for political inferences, whether we intend to allow that or not. The data becomes a mode of political participation we can't fully control. We don't know who has it, can't influence how it is used, and have no say in its distribution. Indeed, generating data is a much more frequent and rich mode of political participation than voting for many modern citizens. It often happens second by second, on multiple devices, enabling constant inferences on a range of subtle issues. By contrast, voting is a relatively simple and basic instrument for expressing your political opinion.

Having built the complex information infrastructure in which we now live, we have less control over how we participate in politics. Or, more accurately, we have surrendered direct, active, and occasional opportunities for blunt expressions of political preference for indirect, passive, and constant surveillance of our nuanced political preferences. Modern citizenship means giving up direct control over the expression of our attitudes and aspirations, because algorithms can infer those things from our behavior. It means surrendering our choice to participate, because we are included in data about political preferences whether we like it or not. We can still choose to participate in some democratic exercises like elections or referenda. But in between those moments of voting we participate, involuntarily, in large data-gathering exercises that probably do more to shape public life—on a rolling basis—than voting.

There are, fortunately, some ways we can individually take back control. More importantly, there are still some ways we can design the system to make us more active, informed participants, with the ability to influence the interpretation of our data once we've generated it. The best election guidelines would create more opportunities for civic expression and more occasions to distribute data across different kinds of political actors and democratic institutions. Getting there requires new flows of data for citizens—opportunities for us to use our data to express our political preferences and support the public organizations and causes we value. We must also develop new democratic practices that take advantage of what is possible on social media platforms. These platforms still afford us some meaningful ways of telling stories, powerful means for building empathy with other citizens, and effective systems for disseminating high-quality information.

Having explored the dark side of public opinion manipulation, technology firms, and political campaigning, you might think that we need to get rid of social media. But the opposite is true. The answer is more social media—not less.

The heart of the problem for public life is that the public opinion data from which we can make political inferences and express ourselves as citizens is overwhelmingly held not by us but by technology firms. Governments have some of the data, but few governments have the capacity to analyze public opinion, relying instead on the tools and services provided by the private sector. Healthy democracies balance power across many political actors: political parties, civil society groups, journalists, private firms, and voters all play crucial roles at different points in the democratic process.

Unfortunately, a lot of civic groups, independent researchers, and working journalists are cut out of the flow of social big data that informs and signals public opinion. To serve members well, civic groups need to know what they need and want. Journalists and academics need to be able to identify and study social problems. Think tanks need data to identify long-term trends and propose policy ideas. Hospitals and charities also need data to provide public health and welfare services effectively. Compared to the big technology firms and political consultants, such groups have significantly less data from which to learn.

A functioning democracy requires that many political actors have some shared understanding of what the political problems are and what the solutions could be. This requires access to shared data. In times past, that meant shared newspapers, which provided a common text that most people, most of the time, had access to. Indeed, for several decades, news organizations have run exit polls during elections in democracies—an important check on the fairness of elections. Journalists exposed gerrymandering, the practice of politicians redrawing electoral boundaries to increase their chances of winning. Now most of the relevant information is held by private firms that profit through the collection, storage, and analysis of big data.

When any one kind of political actor wields too much power, there's trouble. In political science we used to think that the state was defined by having a monopoly on the use of force. Military might was long the primary mechanism of power, but now that mechanism is driven by data. When the ruling elites of authoritarian regimes control all the data about the behavior, attitudes, and aspirations of their people, they wield the strongest and yet most subtle mechanism for social control. Russia and China are good examples of modern states that have an effective monopoly on data about private and public life.

Right now, in most countries around the world, big technology firms hold the largest volumes of the highest-quality data about our private and public lives. They play with information from our social media feeds, credit card purchases, voter registration files, health records, and census details. Increasingly, they work with behavioral data from our mobile phones and the device networks built into our modern homes, computer-enabled cars, and smart cities. Small technology firms feed off this system and take advantage of the algorithms provided by the big social media platforms.

Decades ago, data was more evenly distributed among different kinds of political actors. Governments collected census data, analyzed it to improve public services, and made the data available as a public service. Social scientists ran surveys and made the data available in libraries. Health researchers organized large studies and shared the results. Civic groups, political parties, and unions ran internal votes to understand what their members wanted. Credit card companies and marketing specialists generated consumer data of great value to entrepreneurs. While much of that data was privately held, it was also bought, sold, and traded, and ultimately made more useful when combined with voter registration files or public policy polling data. Large amounts of data on public needs were held by major research organizations like the National Institutes for Health, the Library of Congress, the British Library, and the Bodleian Library.

Now social media firms suck up all that behavioral data—and generate more kinds of data themselves, which they don't share. They certainly profit from it, though, and some of it gets hacked and stolen or simply bought, accessed, or used in some way by authoritarian governments like those of China and Russia. But most governments and civic groups don't share in these troves of knowledge about social problems and public health. To address the concentration of data power among a handful of firms, we must make these firms contribute to public archives like libraries, and we must start helping citizens to express themselves through data donations to the charities and causes they wish to support.

Transparency and Truth Machines

The way to break lie machines is to reassert control over our data and our devices.[12] Or, more accurately, we need to take what we now know about the global political economy that sustains these mechanisms and use that knowledge to insert new opportunities for civic engagement, fresh chances to express ourselves politically, and clear moments in which we can participate in public life by contributing data.

Dismantling lie machines will require new flows of data

between our devices and the public institutions and civic organizations we want to support. Concentrated in a few hands, big data is a threat to democracy. Social media companies and political data-mining firms such as Cambridge Analytica have built their businesses by manipulating public life using personal data. Their work has helped heighten ethnic tensions, revive nationalism, intensify political conflict, and even produce new political crises in countries around the world—all while weakening public trust in journalism, voting systems, and electoral outcomes.

Such crises are symptoms of a deeper problem: the effective monopoly that a handful of technology firms have gained over a wealth of information relevant to public life. Fixing the situation requires putting the public back in charge of data about the public.

Democracy has long been predicated on, and reinforced by, social institutions that carefully collect information about public life and collective needs. Today, however, a handful of technology companies have far exceeded the data-gathering capacity of all other kinds of organizations. These private firms possess detailed information on the public—and having collected and stored data on every user's attitudes, aspirations, and behaviors, they then use it to serve their bottom line. Social media platforms are deliberately designed to exploit the common predilection for selective exposure—the tendency to favor information that confirms preexisting views—to reinforce messaging from advertising clients, lobbyists, political campaign managers, and even foreign governments.

There are two ways to protect democracy from the challenge posed by tech companies' dominance over socially valuable data. The first option is for governments to regulate content on an unprecedented scale. That would oblige public agencies either to review all social media content or to provide clear signals to private firms—whether to the social media companies themselves or to third parties—that they must perform such content reviews. But the problem with these scenarios is that they would create massive new censorship mechanisms that would further threaten democratic culture.

Far preferable would be market regulations that guide firms on how and when they can profit from information about individuals and societies. Such regulations would put the public back in charge of a valuable collective resource while still allowing citizens to express themselves individually by deciding what to do with their data. To get there, policymakers should focus on five basic reforms, all of which would put public institutions back into the flow of data now dominated by private firms.

I've demonstrated that a junk news story is just the most visible component of a much bigger mechanism for tracking and nudging political behavior. By this I mean that the best way to build a data-rich democracy is not to police news content closely, because that would be just treating the symptom. It should be about repairing the flow of data within democracies and should present people with new opportunities for civic engagement and civic expression. Based on what we know about how lie machines work, I think that there are five steps we could take to give ourselves more control over our political futures. Understanding how lie machines work means we can make blueprints for the good mechanisms, clear relationships, and sound evidence we want in our democracy—blueprints that might enable "truth machines."

We need *mandatory reporting on the ultimate beneficiaries of data.* Citizens should easily be able to see which organizations are receiving and manipulating personal data. Social media companies should be able to report back to users on which advertisers, data-mining firms, and political consulting firms have made use of user data. Many people now own consumer products that are part of the internet of things or live in smart cities, where public infrastructure is constantly collecting data about us. If a lobbyist can purchase data about your eating or video watching habits—data collected by the smart refrigerators or televisions you bought for your home— then that equipment should be designed to show you who is using the data and what political inferences they are making about you.

Indeed, governments should require mandatory reporting about the ultimate beneficiaries of data. This means that when queried, technology firms should be required to be transparent in reporting to users which advertisers, data miners, and political consultants have made use of information about them. Your Facebook app or your smart refrigerator should be required to reveal, on request, the list of third parties benefiting from the information the device is collecting. The trail of data should be fully, and clearly, mapped out for users so that if a data-mining firm aggregates users' data and then sells it on to a political party, the users could still identify that ultimate beneficiary. Effectively, this would let you as a citizen see all the parts of the lie machine. Does your data flow through a Chinese government agency? A numbered corporation in Panama? A Polish consulting firm like Imitacja or a Brazilian consulting firm like Imitação? Your devices should reveal such things if so.

A system that allowed for such mandatory reporting could also *allow citizens to donate their data,* selecting additional civic groups to benefit from the flows of information we generate. Data is now the lifeblood of democracy. Social media firms effectively monopolize that data. Not everyone will express themselves this way. But now, and more and more in the future, this would be a wonderful opportunity for civic expression. If a firm monopolizes control of publicly valuable information, democracy is threatened.

Regulations should require social media platforms to facilitate data donation, empowering citizens actively to identify the civic groups, political parties, or research organizations to support. In freeing data from private actors, governments could create an opportunity for civic expression by allowing citizens to share their data with whichever organizations and causes they want to support—not just the ones that can afford to buy it, as is the case today. Lie machines perpetuate political myths and distribute political misinformation. But regulations like these would help small social movements, civic and neighborhood groups, local community actors, and single-issue public society groups to respond to misinformation. Right now, lie machines work so well because social media firms take data about you from you and sell it to people who make political inferences about you. Citizens can significantly weaken those machines by constraining the fuel supply—the personal data—and by sharing this fuel with libraries, independent researchers, and civic groups.

We need an *information infrastructure that tithes*—10 percent of ads on social media platforms should be for public service announcements. Indeed, if we know that a group of people is being targeted with misinformation and being victimized with malign intent, that group could benefit from extra attention from campaigns promoting accurate information and truths. For example, if one segment of the population is being targeted by a voter suppression campaign designed to discourage them from turning up on election day, public agencies could target the same population with clear instructions and encouragement to participate. Ten percent of the data needs to flow (in a secured way) to public health researchers, civil society groups, journalists who do computational journalism, political scientists, and public science agencies like the National Science Foundation and the European Research Council. Such a system would allow many kinds of advocacy groups and public agencies, beyond Facebook's private clients, to use existing data to analyze and solve public problems. One reason lie machines exist is that they are profitable. Someone will always see a business opportunity in running misleading ads and manipulating public information. Directing some of the profits that technology firms make from independent journalism— and some of the data they take from us—back to journalism or into civic groups will restore public life.

Most democracies have rules that prevent firms from profiting from the sale of certain kinds of public data. In many US states, for example, data-mining firms can't profit from the sale of voter registration data, which public agencies collect. *The nonprofit rule regarding data needs to be expanded.* We need to extend this to cover a broader range of data that we would all consider publicly valuable. The kinds of information that most democracies collect as part of a regular census, for example, and information relevant to critical public health and well-being, should be information that firms can't profit from in trading. This rule needs to be extended to a wider range of socially valuable data, such as data that relates to places of employment, which is currently gathered by technology companies. Such classes of information could then be passed to public agencies, thus creating a broader set of data in the public domain. This would also diffuse the financial incentives to build lie machines. A complex system of political intrigue, financial greed, and social media algorithms has weakened our democratic institutions. Technology innovations move fast, and social media platforms are always changing. Making it hard to profit from data mining and misbehaving will discourage people from building new lie machines.

We also need *regular algorithmic audits*. There is no other domain of business in which a company can design and build something, release it onto the market, and change the product only when people complain.

Public agencies should conduct regular audits of social media algorithms and other automated systems that citizens now rely on for information. Technology companies will call these algorithms proprietary and above independent examination. However, public agencies already do audit everything from video gambling machines to financial trading algorithms in ways that don't violate intellectual property. This would allow public officials to inspect and dismantle lie machines on a regular basis. If a social media platform is serving up misinformation at a critical time during an election, it needs to be called out and stopped.

Users should have access to clear explanations of the algorithms that determine what news and advertisements they are exposed to, and those explanations should be confirmed by regular public audits. Moreover, all ads, not just political ones, need to be archived for potential use by public investigators. Audits of today's technology would also put the designers of new technologies—such as artificial intelligence—on notice that they need to anticipate scrutiny.

The Radical Rebuild

Restoring public access to social information wouldn't require legislators to pass a raft of new laws, since most democracies have the public science agencies, libraries, and privacy czars needed to administer large collections of public information effectively. Competition regulators in the European Union and United States may already have the authority to set mandatory guidelines for any technology company with a business model that relies on controlling vast stores of publicly valuable data. Europe's General Data Protection Regulation, which has boldly asserted an individual right to control data since going into effect in May 2018, is an important start. It is already having a global impact, because many technology firms find it easier to implement a platform-wide response than to adjust features for users based in Europe.

Technology firms might claim that such demands would infringe on their economic rights as private enterprises. Yet it's entirely fair to regulate the operations (if not the content) of those firms because the platforms they control have become the fundamental infrastructure for public life. They are a common carrier for our political culture, in much the same way as the post office, newspaper empires, and television and radio broadcasters conveyed politics in past decades.

New initiatives are necessary to tackle junk news and related issues. The risks arising from intervening are not as great as the risks of doing nothing. The market alone can't fix the problem, and so far, industry self-regulation hasn't produced deep changes in the behavior of firms or new habits among users and politicians.

There are certainly big-picture issues that concern societal change. Actors in fields such as education, journalism, and civil society should always pursue and promulgate truths. And it will take international cooperation to dismantle the biggest of lie machines, because as we've seen in this book, the political economy of it all is global. In some instances, the clients paying for a lie machine are in a country other than the providing firms and the target audience.

In an important way, the solution is more social media, not less. We need social media that fulfills the promise—implicit in the term we've given to this family of technologies—that there will be more socialization that happens over this media. These social media platforms can be powerful tools for building empathy and identifying or overcoming problems related to collective action. The advertising and individuated focus of the toolkit, however, doesn't currently provide socialization.

More social media as it is currently designed, however, could be fatal for public life. The social media we need must provide easy access to professionally produced, high-quality political news and information on topics like current events, public health, elections, and major public policy debates. The social media we need must supply socially valuable data to libraries, public agencies, and civil society groups, so that these organizations can work on collectively valued projects. Many collective action problems can be solved with richer data on our attitudes, aspirations, and behavior, and instead of being hoarded by private firms, it should be sitting in shared repositories for and available for analysis. Social media platforms could be the meeting places where thoughtfully structured, representative groups can discuss ideas and arrive at recommendations.

There is a burgeoning amount of evidence that small-group conversation, extended debate, and deliberations among handfuls of citizens produce more informed, reasonable, and actionable outcomes than massive voting exercises.[13] The only way democracy can survive the onslaught of computational propaganda is by correcting this informational imbalance. We probably can't remove social media, but neither can we let it continue in its current form. A radical rebuild could unlock the real potential of social media platforms to support public life.

We shouldn't give up the hope that social media could be dominated by humans, honest citizens, and legitimate voters. Individual political activists expressing themselves through code are not the problem. Problems arise when major organizations of lobbyists, political campaign teams, or foreign governments put lots of resources into developing extensive networks of automated and fake accounts. When candidates for a country's presidency dedicate staff and financial resources to bots, or when big industry lobbyists and large political parties budget for social media manipulation, problems arise. And obviously, even larger problems arise when foreign governments sink resources into shaping public opinion among voters in another country.

These have been significant years for the evolution of lie machines. Major crises in current events and international affairs have revealed the limits of modern democracy and that those limits are currently being set by social media platforms. Social media firms now provide the platforms for our political lives. These technologies permit too much fake news, encourage our herding instincts, and aren't expected to provide public goods. In important ways, social media has provided the mechanism for undermining democratic processes. Misinformation from lobbyists, political campaign teams, or foreign governments can reach millions of voters through the process of production, dissemination, and marketing I have traced out here.

In democracies, citizens expect media companies, journalists, and civic groups to have some public duties, often enforced through the law. Social media and data-mining firms have evaded those responsibilities, hoarding public data with little public oversight. Strengthening democracy and destroying the great lie machines will require putting socially valuable data back to work for the public good.

The war against misinformation is an endless series of small battles. Giving interested citizens the tools to monitor and direct the flow of their data will be fundamental to a future-proof democracy.

Glossary

A/B testing—The process of testing two versions of an ad that differ only in one element (the choice of image or turn of phrase) so that ad designers can compare the conversion rates of each message and make more use of the most compelling version.

Affinity campaigns—Political actors that work together to advance a cause or candidate. Sometimes they share a common plan, but they appear as separate organizations when reporting to elections officials.

Affordances—What you can do with technology, even if designers don't anticipate that activity.

Artificial intelligence (AI)—Collections of algorithms and data that simulate learning, reasoning, and classification.

Astroturfing—The process of seeking electoral victory or legislative relief for grievances by helping political actors find and mobilize a sympathetic public; creating the image of public consensus where there is none.

Authoritarian government—A political system that regularly uses censorship, surveillance, and public opinion manipulation on a wide range of issues and to keep leaders in power.

Big data—Many kinds of information about many people

collected over many types of devices; information that exposes what we do rather than just what we say or think.

Bot or botnet—From *robot* and *network,* a collection of programs that communicate across multiple devices to perform tasks.

Computational propaganda—Misleading news and information, algorithmically generated or distributed, that is served by social media firms to their users.

Conversion rate—The proportion of the audience that clicks on an online advertisement and moves through to a deeper level of engagement.

Core data—Along with demographics such as age, gender, and race, a basic set of facts about who an individual is, where they've been, and what they've been doing.

Cyberattack—The process of finding and exploiting vulnerable device networks by entering them and copying, exporting, or changing the data within them.

Cyberwar—Conflict involving the professional staff of established militaries who no longer just act in response to offline events but are trained to respond to a cyberattack.

Democratic government—A political system in which censorship, surveillance, and public opinion manipulation occurs on a select number of critical issues, with oversight by courts or elected officials, and generally not in order to keep leaders in power. Democracy occurs when the rules and norms of mass surveillance have been developed openly and state practices are acknowledged by the government.

Device tithe—The practice of reserving 10 percent of processing power, data, sensor time, bandwidth, or other network-device feature for users voluntarily and openly to assign to the civic organizations of their choice.

Disinformation—Information that is purposefully crafted

and strategically placed to deceive others—to trick them—into believing a lie or taking action that serves someone else's political interests.

Elective affinity—Our preference for and cognitive bias toward friends, family, people, organizations, and political figures that are in the communities we currently inhabit, are easy to connect to through social networks, and help us avoid the uncertainties of brokering new relationships.

Ideology—Meaning in the service of power. Today, information technology is the most important tool for servicing power.

Impressions—Industry term for the total number of times an ad or post is displayed on a user's screen.

Institutions—Norms, rules, and patterns of behavior.

Internet of things—Networks of manufactured goods with embedded power supplies, small sensors, and an address on the internet. Most of these networked devices are everyday items that are sending and receiving data about their conditions and our behavior.

Junk news—Political news and information that is sensational, extremist, conspiratorial, severely biased, or commentary presented as news.

Legend—The biographical background, supported by a stream of photos, comments, and online activity, that makes an account appear to represent a genuinely social, real person.

Lie machine—The mechanism for putting an untrue claim into service for a political ideology, using social and technical systems that produce, disseminate, and market junk news.

Microtargeting—The process of preparing and delivering customized messages to voters or consumers. Contemporary microtargeting involves preparing and delivering a

message that is customized for particular individuals using
their data, social ties, cognitive biases, and big data records,
often in ways that are unsupervised, untraceable, and
unaccountable and unknown to the individuals.

Misinformation—Contested information that reflects
political disagreement and deviation from expert consensus, scientific knowledge, or lived experience.

Onboarding—An industry term for the process by which
political sympathizers are turned into committed supporters of, donors to, and volunteers for a campaign.

Pax technica—A political, economic, and cultural arrangement of institutions and networked devices in which
government and industry are tightly bound in mutual
defense pacts, design collaborations, standards setting,
and data mining.

Political redlining—The process of deciding which people a
campaign *doesn't* need to engage with, usually with data
about their interest in politics, so that the candidate or
special interest group wastes no resources on communication with unsympathetic citizens.

Push polling—An insidious form of negative campaigning
that plants misinformation and doubt with citizens under
the pretense of running an opinion poll.

Raw data—An industry term for information that has not
been processed or aggregated in some way.

Selective exposure—Our preference for and cognitive bias
toward political news and information that fits an ideology
we subscribe to, is consistent with things we already know,
or helps us avoid the work of rethinking our assumptions.

Sociotechnical system—An organization distinguished by
the relationships between people and devices.

Trolls—Organized teams of people dedicated to manipulating users of social media platforms.

Notes

1
The Science and Technology of Lie Machines

1. Shearer, "Social Media Outpaces Print."
2. Wertime, "Meet the Chinese Trolls."
3. Porup, "Mexican Twitter Bots."
4. Reporters Without Borders, "Vietnam's 'Cyber-Troop' Announcement."
5. Gilbert, "Thailand's Government."
6. Desjardins, "How Much Data?"
7. Kreiss, *Taking Our Country Back.*
8. Howard and Hussain, *Democracy's Fourth Wave?*
9. Hussain and Howard, *State Power 2.0.*
10. Howard, *New Media Campaigns.*
11. Gladwell, "Small Change."
12. Shirky, "Political Power of Social Media."
13. Morozov, *To Save Everything, Click Here;* Pariser, *Filter Bubble.*
14. Howard, *Pax Technica.*
15. Howard, *New Media Campaigns.*
16. Howard and Hussain, *Democracy's Fourth Wave?*
17. Shirky, "Political Power of Social Media."
18. Howard et al., "Sourcing and Automation of Political News and Information"; Neudert et al., "Sourcing and Automation of Political News."
19. Howard et al., "Social Media, News and Political Information."
20. Fourney et al., "Geographic and Temporal Trends in Fake News Consumption."
21. Woolley and Guilbeault, "Computational Propaganda in the United States."

22. Gallacher et al., "Junk News on Military Affairs."

23. Narayanan et al., "Polarization, Partisanship and Junk News."

24. Bradshaw and Howard, "Global Disinformation Order."

25. Jack, "Lexicon of Lies."

26. Marwick and Lewis, "Media Manipulation and Disinformation Online."

27. Jowett and O'Donnell, *Propaganda and Persuasion.*

28. Bradshaw and Howard, "Challenging Truth and Trust," 1.

29. Bradshaw and Howard, "Global Organization of Social Media Disinformation."

30. Bolsover and Howard, "Computational Propaganda and Political Big Data"; Woolley and Howard, *Computational Propaganda.*

31. Bolsover and Howard, "Computational Propaganda and Political Big Data."

32. Woolley and Howard, "Political Communication, Computational Propaganda."

33. Woolley and Howard, *Computational Propaganda.*

34. Turkle, *Alone Together.*

35. Jamieson, *Cyberwar.*

36. Benkler, Faris, and Roberts, *Network Propaganda.*

2

Production

1. Bradshaw and Howard, "Troops, Trolls and Troublemakers."

2. Bradshaw and Howard, "Challenging Truth and Trust"; Bradshaw and Howard, "Troops, Trolls and Troublemakers"; Bradshaw and Howard, "The Global Disinformation Order."

3. Woolley and Howard, "Political Communication, Computational Propaganda, and Autonomous Agents."

4. Howard and Hussain, *Democracy's Fourth Wave?*

5. Howard and Hussain, *Democracy's Fourth Wave?*

6. Howard, *Digital Origins of Dictatorship;* Henisz, Zelner, and Guillen, "Worldwide Diffusion"; Haas, *Saving the Mediterranean.*

7. Hussain and Howard, *State Power 2.0.*

8. Howard, *Digital Origins of Dictatorship;* Howard and Hussain, *Democracy's Fourth Wave?*

9. Howard, Agarwal, and Hussain, "Dictators' Digital Dilemma."

10. Hussain and Howard, *State Power 2.0.*

11. Kremlin [attrib.], *[Assignments for Savushkin 55].*

12. Kurowska and Reshetnikov, "Neutrollization"; Sanovich, "Russia"; Asmolov, "Dynamics of Power"; Jamieson, *Cyberwar.*

13. Sanovich, "Russia."

14. Howard et al., "IRA and Political Polarization."

15. Shane and Goel, "Fake Russian Facebook Accounts."

16. Rankin, "Catalan Independence."

17. Howard et al., "IRA and Political Polarization."

18. "Trust: The Truth?"

19. Brunton, *Spam.*

20. Bradshaw and Howard, "Global Organization of Social Media Disinformation."

3
Distribution

1. Guilbeault and Gorwa, "Tinder Nightmares."

2. Rasmussen, "There Was a Tinder Election Bot."

3. Greenwood, Perrin, and Duggan, "Social Media Update 2016."

4. Howard and Hussain, *Democracy's Fourth Wave?*

5. Sanovich, "Russia."

6. Arnaudo, "Brazil."

7. Gallacher et al., "Junk News on Military Affairs"; Narayanan et al., "Polarization, Partisanship and Junk News."

8. Woolley and Howard, "Political Communication, Computational Propaganda, and Autonomous Agents."

9. Howard, *Pax Technica.*

10. American Association of Public Opinion Researchers, "Problem of So-Called 'Push Polls.'"

11. Howard, Woolley, and Calo, "Algorithms, Bots, and Political Communication."

12. Howard, *Pax Technica.*

13. Qtiesh, "Spam Bots Flooding Twitter"; Ungerleider, "Behind the Mystery of Spam Tweets."

14. "Who Is Using EGHNA Media Server."

15. Scott-Railton and Marquis-Boire, "Call to Harm."

16. Solon, "Syria's White Helmets."

17. Chen, "Cambridge Analytica."

18. Mazzetti et al., "Rick Gates Sought Online Manipulation Plans."

19. Howard, *New Media Campaigns;* Howard, Carr, and Milstein, "Digital Technology."

20. Shane and Goel, "Fake Russian Facebook Accounts."

21. Shane and Goel, "Fake Russian Facebook Accounts"; US Senate, Select Committee on Intelligence, "Testimony of Sean J. Edgett."

22. Isaac and Wakabayashi, "Russian Influence Reached 126 Million."

23. Howard, Woolley, and Calo, "Algorithms, Bots, and Political Communication."

24. Kollanyi, Howard, and Woolley, "Bots and Automation over Twitter."

25. Howard, "How Political Campaigns Weaponize Social Media Bots"; Woolley and Guilbeault, "Computational Propaganda in the United States."

26. Allcott and Gentzkow, "Social Media and Fake News."

27. Howard et al., "Social Media, News and Political Information."

28. Shane and Blinder, "Secret Experiment."

29. "Venezuela Ruling Party"; Pham, "Vietnam Admits Deploying Bloggers."

30. Greenwald, "Hacking Online Polls and Other Ways British Spies Seek to Control the Internet."

31. Weiwei, "China's Paid Trolls."

32. Rueda, "2012's Biggest Social Media Blunders"; Morla, "Ecuador's Correa Recruits Legion"; Morla, "Correa's Social-Media Troll Center."

33. Monaco, "Taiwan"; "Free Tibet Exposes #ChinaSpam"; Kaiman, "Free Tibet Exposes Fake Twitter Accounts."

34. "US Secretly Created 'Cuban Twitter.' "

35. Qtiesh, "Spam Bots Flooding Twitter."

36. Bradshaw and Howard, "Challenging Truth and Trust."

37. Terry, "Twitter's Huge Bot Problem"; US Senate, Select Committee on Intelligence, "Testimony of Sean J. Edgett"; Timberg and Dwoskin, "Twitter Is Sweeping Out Fake Accounts"; Wojcik et al., "Bots in the Twittersphere."

38. Howard, *Pax Technica*.

39. Schreckinger, "Inside Trump's 'Cyborg' Twitter Army."

4
Marketing

1. Lappano et al., "Lauric Acid-Activated Signaling."

2. "Doc Didn't Say Coconut Water Cures Cancer."

3. Fischer, "Russian Efforts to Sow Discord"; Broad, "Your 5G Phone Won't Hurt You."

4. Jensen, "Trump Remains Unpopular."

5. YouGov and *The Economist*, "*The Economist*/YouGov Poll."

6. Sherman, "Poll."

7. Marwick and Lewis, "Media Manipulation and Disinformation Online."

8. Gorwa, "Poland."

9. Daedalus, Field interview, Poland.

10. Maria, Field interview, Brazil.

11. Dwoskin and Timberg, "How Merchants Use Facebook."

12. Maria, Field interview, Brazil.

13. Dhiraj Murthy et al., "Bots and Political Influence."

14. Howard, *New Media Campaigns*.

15. Gragnani, "Inside the World"; Arnaudo, "Brazil."

16. Arnaudo, "Brazil."

17. Banks and Yuki, "O cenário das redes sociais e métricas."

18. We Are Social, "Digital in 2017"; Newman, Levy, and Nielsen, "Reuters Institute Digital News Report 2017."

19. Brasil Liker.

20. Filho and Galhardo, "Governo cita uso de robôs."

21. Aragão, "Eu, robô."

22. Umpierre, "Dilma vai à justiça"; "Altera as leis do código eleitoral."

23. Maria, Field interview, Brazil.

24. "WhatsApp Bans Hundreds of Thousands"; Nalon, "Opinion."

25. Arnaudo, "Brazil."

26. Schmidt, "Estudo mostra que menções a Crivella."

27. Couto, "Estratégico na disputa eleitoral."

28. "Fake News Machine."

29. Arnaudo, "Brazil"; Gorwa, "Poland."

30. Arnaudo, "Brazil."

31. Ortellado and Soltano, "Nova direita nas ruas?"

32. Albuquerque, "Eleição no Rio."

33. Desidério, "7 boatos da política brasileira."

34. Quattrociocchi, Scala, and Sunstein, "Echo Chambers on Facebook"; Flaxman, Goel, and Rao, "Filter Bubbles, Echo Chambers, and Online News Consumption."

35. Chaffee and Miyo, "Selective Exposure and Reinforcement Hypothesis"; Bennett and Iyengar, "New Era of Minimal Effects?"; Iyengar and Hahn, "Red Media, Blue Media"; Fletcher and Nielsen, "Are People Incidentally Exposed"; Dubois and Blank, "The Echo Chamber is Overstated."

36. Lazarsfeld, Berelson, and Gaudet, *People's Choice*.

37. Chaffee and Miyo, "Selective Exposure and Reinforcement Hypothesis."

38. Berelson and Steiner, *Human Behavior*.

39. Fiske, Kinder, and Larter, "Novice and Expert."

40. Fiske, Lau, and Smith, "Varieties and Utilities of Political Expertise"; Ossoff and Dalto, "Media Use and Political Commitment."

41. Cotton and Hieser, "Selective Exposure to Information and Cognitive Dissonance"; Cotton, "Cognitive Dissonance in Selective Exposure."

42. Westen, *Political Brain.*

43. Davis and Jurgenson, "Context Collapse."

44. Chaffee and Miyo, "Selective Exposure and Reinforcement Hypothesis."

45. Chaffee and Miyo, "Selective Exposure and Reinforcement Hypothesis."

46. Bond and Messing, "Quantifying Social Media's Political Space."

47. Gayo-Avello, "Meta-Analysis of State-of-the-Art Electoral Prediction."

48. Bond et al., "61-Million-Person Experiment," 1; Brand, "Can Facebook Influence an Election Result?"; Kramer, Guillory, and Hancock, "Experimental Evidence of Massive-Scale Emotional Contagion."

49. Bakshy, Messing, and Adamic, "Exposure to Ideologically Diverse News and Opinion."

50. Bakshy, Messing, and Adamic, "Exposure to Ideologically Diverse News and Opinion."

51. Fazio, "Unbelievable News?"; Fazio et al., "Knowledge Does Not Protect against Illusory Truth."

52. Bakshy, Messing, and Adamic, "Exposure to Ideologically Diverse News and Opinion"; Messing and Westwood, "Selective Exposure in the Age of Social Media."

53. Epstein and Robertson, "Search Engine Manipulation Effect."

54. Howard, *New Media Campaigns;* Howard, "Digitizing the Social Contract."

55. Phillips, *This Is Why We Can't Have Nice Things.*

56. Diakopoulos, *Automating the News;* Bucher, *If . . . Then.*

57. Confessore et al., "Follower Factory"; Facebook, "Community Standards Enforcement Report."

5
Tracing Impact and Influence

1. Mod, "Facebook-Loving Farmers of Myanmar."

2. McLaughlin, "How Facebook's Rise Fueled Chaos"; Stevenson, "Facebook Admits It Was Used."

3. Mozur, "Genocide Incited on Facebook."

4. Fiveash, "Zuckerberg Claims."

5. Allcott and Gentzkow, "Social Media and Fake News."

6. Spenkuch and Toniatti, "Political Advertising and Election Outcomes."

7. Brader, "Striking a Responsive Chord."

8. Bright et al., "Does Campaigning on Social Media Make a Difference?"

9. Brooks and Geer, "Beyond Negativity"; Malloy and Pearson-Merkowitz, "Going Positive."

10. Fridkin and Kenney, "Variability in Citizens' Reactions."

11. Howard, *New Media Campaigns.*

12. Howard, *New Media Campaigns,* 132.

13. Howard et al., "IRA and Political Polarization"; Silverman, "This Analysis."

14. Some early examples of studies by Facebook staff and their contract researchers include experiments causing mood shifts (Kramer, Guillory, and Hancock, "Experimental Evidence of Massive-Scale Emotional Contagion") and experiments causing changes in political participation (Bond et al., "61-Million-Person Experiment"). Indeed, since the publication of these studies revealed their own assessment of their ability to influence the public, social media firms have been reluctant to share data or collaborate with outside researchers.

15. Howard, *New Media Campaigns.*

16. Howard, Carr, and Milstein, "Digital Technology."

17. The URL for this website is https://tosdr.org/.

18. Perlroth, Tsang, and Satariano, "Marriott Hacking Exposes Data."

19. Erickson and Howard, "Case of Mistaken Identity?"; Howard and Gulyas, "Data Breaches in Europe."

20. Crouch, "Impact of Brexit on Consumer Behaviour."

21. Cummings, "On the Referendum #22."

22. Shipman, *All Out War,* 407.

23. Shipman, *All Out War,* 413–14.

24. Shipman, *All Out War,* 413–14.

25. Cummings, "On the Referendum #21."

26. "UK Statistics Authority Statement on the Use of Official Statistics on Contributions to the European Union."

27. Facebook, Ads supplied by Facebook.

28. Howard, *New Media Campaigns.*

29. Howard, *New Media Campaigns.*

30. The commission found that "Mr. Halsall and Vote Leave both com-

mitted offences under section 118(2)(c) PPERA. Mr. Halsall incurred spending of £449,079 which he knew or ought reasonably to have known was in excess of the statutory spending limit for Vote Leave. The Commission has fined Vote Leave £20,000 for this." This was because the commission was satisfied beyond reasonable doubt that all of Grimes's and BeLeave's spending on referendum campaigning was incurred under a common plan with Vote Leave. Regarding the BeLeave organization, the commission concluded: "The Commission has determined that Mr. Darren Grimes committed an offence under section 117(3) PPERA, and BeLeave committed an offence under section 117(4). Mr. Grimes incurred spending on behalf of BeLeave which he knew or ought reasonably to have known exceeded by £666,016 the statutory limit for a non-registered campaigner. The Commission has fined Mr. Grimes £20,000 for this." Electoral Commission, "Report of an Investigation," 8.

31. On June 22, 2016, £1 was worth $1.4795. In US dollars, then, Vote Leave's total excess spending was $664,412.

32. Electoral Commission, "Report of an Investigation."

33. Facebook, Ads supplied by Facebook.

34. Electoral Commission, "Report of an Investigation."

35. Stimson, "Letter Dated 19 July 2018."

36. Cummings, "On the Referendum #22."

37. Corbyn, "Facebook Experiment Boosts US Voter Turnout."

38. Grassegger and Krogerus, "Data That Turned the World Upside Down."

6
Future-Proof Solutions for a Data-Rich Democracy

1. Jowett and O'Donnell, *Propaganda and Persuasion.*

2. Bradshaw, Neudert, and Howard, "Government Responses to Malicious Use of Social Media"; Taylor, Walsh, and Bradshaw, "Industry Responses to Malicious Use of Social Media."

3. Bennett and Iyengar, "New Era of Minimal Effects?"

4. Woolley and Howard, *Computational Propaganda.*

5. Miller, "Can an Algorithm Hire Better Than a Human?"; Mann and O'Neil, "Hiring Algorithms Are Not Neutral."

6. Howard, *Pax Technica.*

7. Howard, *New Media Campaigns.*

8. Howard, *Pax Technica.*

9. "Internet of Things."

10. "Gartner Says the Internet of Things Installed Base Will Grow"; ABI

Research, "More Than 30 Billion Devices"; "Internet of Things"; "Space"; OECD, "Building Blocks for Smart Networks."

11. Andrejevic, *Infoglut.*
12. Howard, "Our Data, Ourselves."
13. Fishkin and Diamond, "This Experiment Has Some Great News."

Bibliography

ABI Research. "More Than 30 Billion Devices Will Wirelessly Connect to the Internet of Everything in 2020." May 9, 2013. https://www.abiresearch.com/press/more-than-30-billion-devices-will-wirelessly-conne/.

Albuquerque, Ana Luiza. "Eleição no Rio tem tática 'antiboato' e suspeita de uso de robôs [Election in Rio has 'anti-bull' tactics and suspected use of robots]." *Folha de São Paulo* (blog), October 18, 2016. http://www1.folha.uol.com.br/poder/eleicoes-2016/2016/10/1823713-eleicao-no-rio-tem-tatica-antiboato-e-suspeita-de-uso-de-robos.shtml.

Allcott, Hunt, and Matthew Gentzkow. "Social Media and Fake News in the 2016 Election." *Journal of Economic Perspectives* 31, no. 2 (Spring 2017): 211–36. https://doi.org/10.1257/jep.31.2.211.

American Association of Public Opinion Researchers. "AAPOR Statements on 'Push' Polls." June 2007, updated October 2015. https://www.aapor.org/Standards-Ethics/Resources/AAPOR-Statements-on-Push-Polls.aspx.

Andrejevic, Mark. *Infoglut: How Too Much Information Is Changing the Way We Think and Know.* New York: Routledge, 2013.

Aragão, A. "Eu, robô [I robot]." *Folha de São Paulo* (blog), September 30, 2014. https://www1.folha.uol.com.br/fsp/especial/188299-eu-robo.shtml.

Arnaudo, Dan. "Brazil: Political Bot Intervention during Pivotal Events." In *Computational Propaganda: Political Parties, Politicians, and Political Manipulation on Social Media,* edited by Samuel C. Woolley and Philip N. Howard, 128–52. New York: Oxford University Press, 2019.

Asmolov, Gregory. "Dynamics of Power and the Balance of Power in Russia." In *State Power 2.0: Authoritarian Entrenchment and Political Engagement Worldwide,* edited by Muzammil M. Hussain and Philip N. Howard, 139–52. London: Ashgate, 2013.

Bakshy, Eytan, Solomon Messing, and Lada A. Adamic. "Exposure to Ideo-logically Diverse News and Opinion on Facebook." *Science* 348, no. 6239 (2015): 1130–32. https://doi.org/10.1126/science.aaa1160.

Banks, Alex, and Tania Yuki. "O cenário das redes sociais e métricas que real-mente importam [The social and metric networks scenario that really matters]." ComScore, Inc., September 16, 2014. http://www.comscore.com /por/Insights/Presentations-and-Whitepapers/2014/The-State-of -Social-Media-in-Brazil-and-the-Metrics-that-Really-Matter.

Benkler, Yochai, Robert Faris, and Hal Roberts. *Network Propaganda: Ma-nipulation, Disinformation, and Radicalization in American Politics.* New York: Oxford University Press, 2018.

Bennett, W. Lance, and Shanto Iyengar. "A New Era of Minimal Effects? The Changing Foundations of Political Communication." *Journal of Commu-nication* 58, no. 4 (2008): 707–31. https://doi.org/10.1111/j.1460-2466.2008 .00410.x.

Berelson, Bernard, and Gary A. Steiner. *Human Behavior: An Inventory of Scientific Findings.* Oxford: Harcourt, Brace and World, 1964.

Bolsover, Gillian, and Philip Howard. "Computational Propaganda and Po-litical Big Data: Moving toward a More Critical Research Agenda." *Big Data* 5, no. 4 (2017): 273–76. https://doi.org/10.1089/big.2017.29024.cpr.

Bond, Robert, and Solomon Messing. "Quantifying Social Media's Political Space: Estimating Ideology from Publicly Revealed Preferences on Face-book." *American Political Science Review* 109, no. 1 (2015): 62–78. https:// doi.org/10.1017/S0003055414000525.

Bond, Robert M., et al. "A 61-Million-Person Experiment in Social Influence and Political Mobilization." *Nature* 489, no. 7415 (September 13, 2012): 295–98. https://doi.org/10.1038/nature11421.

Brader, Ted. "Striking a Responsive Chord: How Political Ads Motivate and Persuade Voters by Appealing to Emotions." *American Journal of Political Science* 49, no. 2 (2005): 388–405. https://doi.org/10.1111/j.0092-5853.2005 .00130.x.

Bradshaw, Samantha, and Philip N. Howard. "Challenging Truth and Trust: A Global Inventory of Organized Social Media Manipulation." Working Paper No. 2018.1. Project on Computational Propaganda, Oxford Inter-net Institute, Oxford University, July 2018. https://comprop.oii.ox.ac.uk /research/cybertroops2018/.

———. "The Global Disinformation Order: A Global Inventory of Orga-nized Social Media Manipulation." Working Paper No. 2019.2. Project on Computational Propaganda, Oxford Internet Institute, Oxford University, September 2019. https://comprop.oii.ox.ac.uk/research/cybertroops2019/.

———. "The Global Organization of Social Media Disinformation Campaigns." *Journal of International Affairs* 71, no. 1.5 (September 17, 2018): 23–32. https://jia.sipa.columbia.edu/global-organization-social-media-dis information-campaigns.

———. "Troops, Trolls and Troublemakers: A Global Inventory of Organized Social Media Manipulation." Working Paper No. 2017.12. Project on Computational Propaganda, Oxford Internet Institute, Oxford University, July 2017. https://comprop.oii.ox.ac.uk/wp-content/uploads/sites /89/2017/07/Troops-Trolls-and-Troublemakers.pdf.

Bradshaw, Samantha, Lisa-Maria Neudert, and Philip N. Howard. "Government Responses to Malicious Use of Social Media." Working Paper No. 2019.2. Project on Computational Propaganda, Oxford Internet Institute, Oxford University, November 2019. https://comprop.oii.ox.ac.uk/research /government-responses/.

Brand, Michael. "Can Facebook Influence an Election Result?" *The Conversation,* September 27, 2016. http://theconversation.com/can-facebook -influence-an-election-result-65541.

Brasil Liker. 2019. https://brasilliker.com.br/.

Bright, Jonathan, et al. "Does Campaigning on Social Media Make a Difference? Evidence from Candidate Use of Twitter during the 2015 and 2017 UK Elections." *Communication Research* 47, no. 1 (2019): 122. https://doi .org/10.1177/0093650219872394.

Broad, William J. "Your 5G Phone Won't Hurt You. But Russia Wants You to Think Otherwise." *New York Times,* May 12, 2019. https://www.nytimes .com/2019/05/12/science/5g-phone-safety-health-russia.html.

Brooks, Deborah Jordan, and John G. Geer. "Beyond Negativity: The Effects of Incivility on the Electorate." *American Journal of Political Science* 51, no. 1 (2007): 1–16. https://doi.org/10.1111/j.1540-5907.2007.00233.x.

Bucher, Taina. *If . . . Then: Algorithmic Power and Politics.* New York: Oxford University Press, 2018.

Brunton, Finn. *Spam: A Shadow History of the Internet.* Cambridge, MA: MIT Press, 2013.

Chaffee, Steven H., and Yuko Miyo. "Selective Exposure and the Reinforcement Hypothesis: An Intergenerational Panel Study of the 1980 Presidential Campaign." *Communication Research* 10, no. 1 (1983): 3–36. https:// doi.org/10.1177/009365083010001001.

Chen, Adrian. "Cambridge Analytica and Our Lives inside the Surveillance Machine." *New Yorker,* March 21, 2018. https://www.newyorker.com/tech /annals-of-technology/cambridge-analytica-and-our-lives-inside-the -surveillance-machine.

Confessore, Nicholas, Gabriel J. X. Dance, Richard Harris, and Mark Hansen. "The Follower Factory." *New York Times,* January 27, 2018. https://

www.nytimes.com/interactive/2018/01/27/technology/social-media
-bots.html.

Corbyn, Zoe. "Facebook Experiment Boosts US Voter Turnout." *Nature News,* September 12, 2012. https://doi.org/10.1038/nature.2012.11401.

Cotton, John. "Cognitive Dissonance in Selective Exposure." In *Selective Exposure to Communication,* edited by Dolf Zillmann, 11–34. New York: Routledge, 2013.

Cotton, John L., and Rex A. Hieser. "Selective Exposure to Information and Cognitive Dissonance." *Journal of Research in Personality* 14, no. 4 (1980): 518–27. https://doi.org/10.1016/0092-6566(80)90009-4.

Couto, Marlen. "Estratégico na disputa eleitoral, WhatsApp deve ter efeito inesperado [Strategic in the electoral contest, WhatsApp must have an unexpected effect]." *O Globo,* August 15, 2016. https://oglobo.globo.com /brasil/estrategico-na-disputa-eleitoral-whatsapp-deve-ter-efeito-in esperado-19923064.

Crouch, James. "Impact of Brexit on Consumer Behaviour." *Opinium Research,* 2016. https://www.opinium.co.uk/impact-of-brexit-on-consumer -behaviour/.

Cummings, Dominic. "On the Referendum #21: Branching Histories of the 2016 Referendum and 'The Frogs before the Storm.'" *Dominic Cummings's Blog* (blog), January 9, 2017. https://dominiccummings.com/2017 /01/09/on-the-referendum-21-branching-histories-of-the-2016-referendum -and-the-frogs-before-the-storm-2/.

———. "On the Referendum #22: Some Basic Numbers for the Vote Leave Campaign." *Dominic Cummings' Blog* (blog), January 30, 2017. https:// dominiccummings.files.wordpress.com/2017/01/20170130-referendum -22-numbers.pdf.

Daedalus. Field interview, Poland, by Robert Gorwa, September 1, 2016. Project on Computational Propaganda, Oxford Internet Institute, Oxford University.

Davis, Jenny L., and Nathan Jurgenson. "Context Collapse: Theorizing Context Collusions and Collisions." *Information, Communication and Society* 17, no. 4 (April 21, 2014): 476–85. https://doi.org/10.1080/1369118X.2014 .888458.

Desjardins, Jeff. "How Much Data Is Generated Each Day?" *World Economic Forum,* April 17, 2019. https://www.weforum.org/agenda/2019/04/how -much-data-is-generated-each-day-cf4bddf29f/.

Desidério, Mariana. "7 boatos da política brasileira que podem ter enganado você [7 rumors of Brazilian politics that may have deceived you]." *Exame,* September 13, 2016. http://exame.abril.com.br/brasil/7-boatos-da-politica -brasileiraque-podem-ter-enganado-voce/.

Diakopoulos, Nicholas. *Automating the News: How Algorithms Are Rewriting the Media.* Cambridge, MA: Harvard University Press, 2019.

"Doc Didn't Say Coconut Water Cures Cancer." *Hindustan Times,* May 18, 2019. https://www.hindustantimes.com/mumbai-news/doc-didn-t-say -coconut-water-cures-cancer/story-WilJiWr9VES56tFxtOLMNM.html.

Dubois, Elizabeth and Grant Blank. "The Echo Chamber is Overstated: The Moderating Effect of Political Interest and Diverse Media." *Information, Communication & Society* 21, no. 5 (2018): 729–745. https://doi.org//10.1080 /1369118X.2018.1428656.

Dwoskin, Elizabeth, and Craig Timberg. "How Merchants Use Facebook to Flood Amazon with Fake Reviews." *Washington Post,* April 23, 2018. https://www.washingtonpost.com/business/economy/how-merchants -secretly-use-facebook-to-flood-amazon-with-fake-reviews/2018/04/23 /5dad1e30-4392-11e8-8569-26fda6b404c7_story.html.

The Electoral Commission. "Report of an Investigation in Respect of: Vote Leave Limited, Mr. Darren Grimes, BeLeave, Veterans for Britain." July 17, 2018. https://www.electoralcommission.org.uk/who-we-are-and-what-we -do/our-enforcement-work/investigations/investigation-vote-leave -ltd-mr-darren-grimes-beleave-and-veterans-britain.

Epstein, Robert, and Ronald E. Robertson. "The Search Engine Manipulation Effect (SEME) and Its Possible Impact on the Outcomes of Elections." *Proceedings of the National Academy of Sciences* 112, no. 33 (2015): E4512–21. https://doi.org/10.1073/pnas.1419828112.

Erickson, Kris, and Philip N. Howard. "A Case of Mistaken Identity? News Accounts of Hacker, Consumer, and Organizational Responsibility for Compromised Digital Records." *Journal of Computer-Mediated Communication* 12, no. 4 (2007): 1229–47. https://doi.org/10.1111/j.1083-6101.2007 .00371.x.

Facebook. Ads supplied by Facebook to the DCMS Committee (2018). https://www.parliament.uk/documents/commons-committees/culture -media-and-sport/Fake_news_evidence/Ads-supplied-by-Facebook-to -the-DCMS-Committee.pdf.

———. "Community Standards Enforcement Report." May 2019. https:// transparency.facebook.com/community-standards-enforcement.

"The Fake News Machine: Inside a Town Gearing Up for 2020." *CNN Money,* 2017. https://money.cnn.com/interactive/media/the-macedonia-story/.

Fazio, Lisa. "Unbelievable News? Read It Again and You Might Think It's True." *The Conversation,* December 5, 2016. http://theconversation.com /unbelievable-news-read-it-again-and-you-might-think-its-true-69602.

Fazio, Lisa K., Nadia M. Brashier, B. Keith Payne, and Elizabeth J. Marsh. "Knowledge Does Not Protect against Illusory Truth." *Journal of Experi-*

mental Psychology. General 144, no. 5 (October 2015): 993–1002. https://doi.org/10.1037/xge0000098.

Filho, V. H., and R. Galhardo. "Governo cita uso de robôs nas redes sociais em campanha eleitoral [Government citation use of robots in social networks in electoral campaign]." *Estadão de São Paulo,* March 17, 2015. http://politica.estadao.com.br/noticias/geral,governo-cita-uso-de-robos-nasredes-sociais-em-campanha-eleitoral,1652771.

Fischer, Sara. "Russian Efforts to Sow Discord ahead of 2020 Elections Appear Focused on Fear-Mongering around Healthcare Issues." *Business Insider,* May 30, 2019. https://www.businessinsider.com/russian-misinformation-efforts-focus-on-healthcare-fear-mongering-2019-5.

Fishkin, James, and Larry Diamond. "This Experiment Has Some Great News for Our Democracy." *New York Times,* October 2, 2019. https://www.nytimes.com/2019/10/02/opinion/america-one-room-experiment.html.

Fiske, Susan T., Donald R. Kinder, and W. Michael Larter. "The Novice and the Expert: Knowledge-Based Strategies in Political Cognition." *Journal of Experimental Social Psychology* 19, no. 4 (1983): 381–400. https://doi.org/10.1016/0022-1031(83)90029-X.

Fiske, Susan T., Richard R. Lau, and Richard A. Smith. "On the Varieties and Utilities of Political Expertise." *Social Cognition* 8, no. 1 (1990): 31–48. https://doi.org/10.1521/soco.1990.8.1.31.

Fiveash, Kelly. "Zuckerberg Claims Just 1% of Facebook Posts Carry Fake News." *Ars Technica,* November 14, 2016. https://arstechnica.com/information-technology/2016/11/zuckerberg-claims-1-percent-facebook-posts-fake-news-trump-election/.

Flaxman, Seth, Sharad Goel, and Justin M. Rao. "Filter Bubbles, Echo Chambers, and Online News Consumption." *Public Opinion Quarterly* 80, no. S1 (2016): 298–320. https://doi.org/10.1093/poq/nfw006.

Fletcher, Richard and Rasmus Kleis Nielsen. "Are People Incidentally Exposed to News on Social Media? A Comparative Analysis." *New Media & Society* 20, no. 7 (2017): 2450–2468/ https://doi.org/10/1177/1461444817724170.

Fourney, Adam, et al. "Geographic and Temporal Trends in Fake News Consumption during the 2016 US Presidential Election." *Proceedings of the 2017 ACM on Conference on Information and Knowledge Management* (November 6, 2017): 2071–74. http://doi.acm.org/10.1145/3132847.3133147.

"Free Tibet Exposes #ChinaSpam on Twitter." *Free Tibet,* July 17, 2014. https://freetibet.org/news-media/na/free-tibet-exposes-chinaspam-twitter.

Fridkin, Kim L., and Patrick J. Kenney. "Variability in Citizens' Reactions to

Different Types of Negative Campaigns." *American Journal of Political Science* 55, no. 2 (2011): 307–25.

Gallacher, John D., Vlad Barash, Philip N. Howard, and John Kelly. "Junk News on Military Affairs and National Security: Social Media Disinformation Campaigns against US Military Personnel and Veterans." Data Memo No. 2017.9. Project on Computational Propaganda, Oxford Internet Institute, Oxford University, October 2017. https://comprop.oii.ox.ac .uk/research/working-papers/vetops/.

"Gartner Says the Internet of Things Installed Base Will Grow to 26 Billion Units by 2020." *Gartner,* 2013. http://www.gartner.com/newsroom/id /2636073.

Gayo-Avello, Daniel. "A Meta-Analysis of State-of-the-Art Electoral Prediction from Twitter Data." *Social Science Computer Review* 2013, 08944 39313493979. https://doi.org/10.1177/0894439313493979.

Gilbert, David. "Thailand's Government Is Using Child 'Cyber Scouts' to Monitor Dissent." *Vice News,* September 20, 2016. https://news.vice.com /article/thailands-royal-family-is-using-child-cyber-scouts-to-monitor -dissent.

Gladwell, Malcolm. "Small Change." *New Yorker,* September 27, 2010. http:// www.newyorker.com/reporting/2010/10/04/101004fa_fact_gladwell.

Gorwa, Robert. "Poland: Unpacking the Ecosystem of Social Media Manipulation." In *Computational Propaganda: Political Parties, Politicians, and Political Manipulation on Social Media,* edited by Samuel C. Woolley and Philip N. Howard, 86–103. New York: Oxford University Press, 2018.

Gragnani, Juliana. "Inside the World of Brazil's Social Media Cyborgs." *BBC News,* December 13, 2017. http://www.bbc.co.uk/news/world-latin-america -42322064.

Grassegger, Hannes, and Mikael Krogerus. "The Data That Turned the World Upside Down." *Motherboard.* https://motherboard.vice.com/en_us/article /how-our-likes-helped-trump-win.

Greenwald, Glenn. "Hacking Online Polls and Other Ways British Spies Seek to Control the Internet." *The Intercept,* July 14, 2014. https://theintercept .com/2014/07/14/manipulating-online-polls-ways-british-spies-seek -control-internet/.

Greenwood, Shannon, Andrew Perrin, and Maeve Duggan. "Social Media Update 2016." Pew Research Center, November 11, 2016. http://www.pew internet.org/2016/11/11/social-media-update-2016/.

Guilbeault, Douglas, and Robert Gorwa. "Tinder Nightmares: The Promise and Peril of Political Bots." *Wired UK,* July 7, 2017. https://www.wired .co.uk/article/tinder-political-bots-jeremy-corbyn-labour.

Haas, Peter M. *Saving the Mediterranean: The Politics of International Environmental Cooperation.* New York: Columbia University Press, 1990.

Henisz, Witold J., Bennet A. Zelner, and Mauro F. Guillén. "The Worldwide Diffusion of Market-Oriented Infrastructure Reform, 1977–1999." *American Sociological Review* 70, no. 6 (2005): 871–97. https://doi.org/10.1177/000312240507000601.

House of Commons. Digital, Culture, Media and Sport Committee. *Disinformation and "Fake News": Interim Report.* UK Parliament, HC 363, July 29, 2018. https://publications.parliament.uk/pa/cm201719/cmselect/cm cumeds/363/363.pdf.

Howard, Philip N. *The Digital Origins of Dictatorship and Democracy: Information Technology and Political Islam.* New York: Oxford University Press, 2011.

———. "Digitizing the Social Contract: Producing American Political Culture in the Age of New Media." *Communication Review* 6, no. 3 (July 1, 2003): 213–45. https://doi.org/10.1080/10714420390226270.

———. "How Political Campaigns Weaponize Social Media Bots." *IEEE Spectrum,* October 18, 2018. https://spectrum.ieee.org/computing/software/how-political-campaigns-weaponize-social-media-bots.

———. *New Media Campaigns and the Managed Citizen.* New York: Cambridge University Press, 2006.

———. "Our Data, Ourselves: How to Stop Tech Firms from Monopolizing Our Personal Information." *Foreign Policy,* July 16, 2018. https://foreignpolicy.com/2018/07/16/our-data-ourselves-democracy-technology-algorithms/.

———. *Pax Technica: How the Internet of Things May Set Us Free or Lock Us Up.* New Haven: Yale University Press, 2015.

Howard, Philip N., and Orsolya Gulyas. "Data Breaches in Europe: Reported Breaches of Compromised Personal Records in Europe, 2005–2014." SSRN Scholarly Paper. Rochester, NY: Social Science Research Network, October 1, 2014. http://dx.doi.org/10.2139/ssrn.2554352.

Howard, Philip N., and Muzammil M. Hussain. *Democracy's Fourth Wave? Digital Media and the Arab Spring.* New York: Oxford University Press, 2013.

Howard, Philip N., Sheetal D. Agarwal, and Muzammil M. Hussain. "The Dictators' Digital Dilemma: When Do States Disconnect Their Digital Networks?" *Brookings Institution,* 2011. https://www.brookings.edu/wp-content/uploads/2016/06/10_dictators_digital_network.pdf.

Howard, Philip N., John N. Carr, and Tema J. Milstein. "Digital Technology and the Market for Political Surveillance." *Surveillance and Society* 3, no. 1 (2002). https://doi.org/10.24908/ss.v3i1.3320.

Howard, Philip N., Samuel Woolley, and Ryan Calo. "Algorithms, Bots, and Political Communication in the US 2016 Election: The Challenge of Automated Political Communication for Election Law and Administration." *Journal of Information Technology and Politics* 15, no. 2 (2018): 81–93. https://doi.org/10.1080/19331681.2018.1448735.

Howard, Philip N., Bence Kollanyi, Samantha Bradshaw, and Lisa Maria Neudert. "Social Media, News and Political Information during the US Election: Was Polarizing Content Concentrated in Swing States?" Data Memo No. 2017.8. Computation Propaganda Project, Oxford Internet Institute, Oxford University, September 2017. https://comprop.oii.ox.ac.uk/research/working-papers/social-media-news-and-political-information-during-the-us-election-was-polarizing-content-concentrated-in-swing-states/.

Howard, Philip N., Lisa-Maria Neudert, Samantha Bradshaw, and Bence Kollanyi. "Sourcing and Automation of Political News and Information over Social Media in the United States, 2016–2018." *Political Communication*, (2019): 1–21. https://doi.org/10.1080/10584609.2019.1663322.

Howard, Philip N., et al. "The IRA and Political Polarization in the United States." Working Paper No. 2018.2. Project on Computational Propaganda, Oxford Internet Institute, Oxford University, December 2018. https://comprop.oii.ox.ac.uk/research/ira-political-polarization/.

Hussain, Muzammil M., and Philip N. Howard. *State Power 2.0: Digital Networks and Authoritarian Rule.* London: Ashgate, 2013.

"The Internet of Things." CISCO IBGS. 2014. https://www.cisco.com/c/dam/en_us/solutions/trends/iot/docs/iot-aag.pdf.

Isaac, Mike, and Daisuke Wakabayashi. "Russian Influence Reached 126 Million through Facebook Alone." *New York Times,* October 30, 2017. https://www.nytimes.com/2017/10/30/technology/facebook-google-russia.html.

Iyengar, Shanto, and Kyu S. Hahn. "Red Media, Blue Media: Evidence of Ideological Selectivity in Media Use." *Journal of Communication* 59, no. 1 (2009): 19–39. https://doi.org/10.1111/j.1460-2466.2008.01402.x.

Jack, Caroline. "Lexicon of Lies: Terms for Problematic Information." Data & Society Research Institute, August 9, 2017. https://datasociety.net/pubs/oh/DataAndSociety_LexiconofLies.pdf.

Jamieson, Kathleen Hall. *Cyberwar: How Russian Hackers and Trolls Helped Elect a President—What We Don't, Can't, and Do Know.* New York: Oxford University Press, 2018.

Jensen, Tom. "Trump Remains Unpopular; Voters Prefer Obama on SCOTUS Pick." *Public Policy Polling,* December 9, 2016. https://www.publicpolicypolling.com/polls/trump-remains-unpopular-voters-prefer-obama-on-scotus-pick/.

Jowett, Garth, and Victoria O'Donnell. *Propaganda and Persuasion.* London: Sage, 1986.

Kaiman, Jonathan. "Free Tibet Exposes Fake Twitter Accounts by China Propagandists." *Guardian,* July 22, 2014. https://www.theguardian.com/world /2014/jul/22/free-tibet-fake-twitter-accounts-china-propagandists.

Kollanyi, Bence, Philip N. Howard, and Samuel C. Woolley. "Bots and Automation over Twitter during the Third U.S. Presidential Debate." Data Memo No. 2016.3. Project on Computational Propaganda, Oxford Internet Institute, Oxford University, October 2016. https://comprop.oii.ox.ac .uk/research/working-papers/bots-and-automation-over-twitter-during -the-third-u-s-presidential-debate/.

Kramer, Adam D. I., Jamie E. Guillory, and Jeffrey T. Hancock. "Experimental Evidence of Massive-Scale Emotional Contagion through Social Networks." *Proceedings of the National Academy of Sciences* 111, no. 24 (June 17, 2014): 8788–90. https://doi.org/10.1073/pnas.1320040111.

Kreiss, Daniel. *Taking Our Country Back: The Crafting of Networked Politics from Howard Dean to Barack Obama.* New York: Oxford University Press, 2012.

Kremlin [attrib.]. [*Assignments for Savushkin 55*]. 2016.

Kurowska, Xymena, and Anatoly Reshetnikov. "Neutrollization: Industrialized Trolling as a Pro-Kremlin Strategy of Desecuritization." *Security Dialogue* 49, no. 5 (2018): 345–63. https://doi.org/10.1177/0967010618785102.

Lappano, Rosamaria, et al. "The Lauric Acid-Activated Signaling Prompts Apoptosis in Cancer Cells." *Cell Death Discovery* 3 (2017). https://doi.org /10.1038/cddiscovery.2017.63.

Lazarsfeld, Paul Felix, Bernard Berelson, and Hazel Gaudet. *The People's Choice: How the Voter Makes Up His Mind in a Presidential Campaign.* New York: Columbia University Press, 1948.

Lytvynenko, Jane. "Here Are Some Job Ads for the Russian Troll Factory." *BuzzFeed,* February 22, 2018. https://www.buzzfeed.com/janelytvynenko /job-ads-for-russian-troll-factory.

Malloy, Liam C., and Shanna Pearson-Merkowitz. "Going Positive: The Effects of Negative and Positive Advertising on Candidate Success and Voter Turnout." *Research and Politics* 3, no. 1 (2016). https://doi.org/10 .1177/2053168015625078.

Maria. Field interview, Brazil, by Daniel Arnaudo, September 1, 2016. Project on Computational Propaganda, Oxford Internet Institute, Oxford University.

Mann, Gideon, and Cathy O'Neil. "Hiring Algorithms Are Not Neutral." *Harvard Business Review,* December 9, 2016. https://hbr.org/2016/12/hiring -algorithms-are-not-neutral.

Marwick, Alice, and Rebecca Lewis. "Media Manipulation and Disinformation Online." Data & Society Research Institute, May 15, 2017. https://
datasociety.net/pubs/oh/DataAndSociety_MediaManipulationAnd
DisinformationOnline.pdf.

Mazzetti, Mark, Ronen Bergman, David D. Kirkpatrick, and Maggie Haber-
man. "Rick Gates Sought Online Manipulation Plans from Israeli Intelligence Firm for Trump Campaign." *New York Times,* October 8, 2018.
https://www.nytimes.com/2018/10/08/us/politics/rick-gates-psy-group
-trump.html.

McLaughlin, Timothy. "How Facebook's Rise Fueled Chaos and Confusion
in Myanmar." *Wired,* July 6, 2018. https://www.wired.com/story/how
-facebooks-rise-fueled-chaos-and-confusion-in-myanmar/.

Messing, Solomon, and Sean J. Westwood. "Selective Exposure in the Age of
Social Media: Endorsements Trump Partisan Source Affiliation When Selecting News Online." *Communication Research* 41, no. 8 (2014): 1042–63.
https://doi.org/10.1177/0093650212466406.

Miller, Claire Cain. "Can an Algorithm Hire Better Than a Human?" *New
York Times,* June 25, 2015. https://www.nytimes.com/2015/06/26/upshot
/can-an-algorithm-hire-better-than-a-human.html.

Mod, Craig. "The Facebook-Loving Farmers of Myanmar." *Atlantic,* January 21, 2016. https://www.theatlantic.com/technology/archive/2016/01
/the-facebook-loving-farmers-of-myanmar/424812/.

Monaco, Nicholas. "Taiwan: Digital Democracy Meets Automated Autoc-
racy." In *Computational Propaganda: Political Parties, Politicians, and Political Manipulation on Social Media,* edited by Samuel C. Woolley and
Philip N. Howard, 104–127. New York: Oxford University Press, 2018.

Morla, Rebeca. "Correa's Social-Media Troll Center Exposed in Quito."
PanAm Post, March 25, 2015. https://panampost.com/rebeca-morla/2015
/03/25/correas-social-media-troll-center-exposed-in-quito/.

———. "Ecuador's Correa Recruits Legion of Social-Media Trolls." *PanAm
Post,* January 26, 2015. https://panampost.com/rebeca-morla/2015/01/26
/ecuadors-correa-recruits-legion-of-social-media-trolls/.

Morozov, Evgeny. *To Save Everything, Click Here: Technology, Solutionism,
and the Urge to Fix Problems That Don't Exist.* New York: PublicAffairs,
2013.

Mozur, Paul. "A Genocide Incited on Facebook, with Posts from Myanmar's
Military." *New York Times,* October 15, 2018. https://www.nytimes.com
/2018/10/15/technology/myanmar-facebook-genocide.html.

Murthy, Dhiraj, et al. "Bots and Political Influence: A Sociotechnical Investigation of Social Network Capital." *International Journal of Communication* 10 (2016): 4952–71.

Nalon, Tai. "Opinion: Did WhatsApp Help Bolsonaro Win the Brazilian Presidency?" *Washington Post,* November 1, 2018. https://www.washington post.com/news/theworldpost/wp/2018/11/01/whatsapp-2/.

Narayanan, Vidya, et al. "Polarization, Partisanship and Junk News Consumption over Social Media in the US." Data Memo No. 2018.1. Project on Computational Propaganda, Oxford Internet Institute, Oxford University, February 2018. https://comprop.oii.ox.ac.uk/research/polarization -partisanship-and-junk-news/.

Neudert, Lisa-Maria, Philip N. Howard, and Bence Kollanyi. "Sourcing and Automation of Political News and Information during Three European Elections." *Social Media + Society 5,* no. 3: 1–13. https://doi.org/10.1177 /2056305119863147.

Newman, Nic, David A. L. Levy, and Rasmus Kleis Nielsen. "Reuters Institute Digital News Report 2017." *SSRN Electronic Journal,* 2015. https://doi .org/10.2139/ssrn.2619576.

"Number of Connected Devices Worldwide, 2015–2025." *Statista.* 2019. https://www.statista.com/statistics/471264/iot-number-of-connected -devices-worldwide/.

OECD. "Building Blocks for Smart Networks." January 17, 2013. https://doi .org/10.1787/5k4dkhvnzv35-en.

Ortellado, Pablo, and Esther Soltano. "Nova direita nas ruas? Uma análise do descompasso entre manifestantes e convocantes dos protestos anti-governo de 2015 [New right on the streets? An analysis of the mismatch between protesters and the protesters of the anti-government protests of 2015]." *História, Memória e Política* 11 (2016): 69–188. http://revistaperseu .fpabramo.org.br/index.php/revista-perseu/article/view/97.

Ossoff, Elizabeth P., and Carol Ann Dalto. "Media Use and Political Commitment: The 1992 U.S. Presidential Election." *Current Psychology* 15, no. 2 (June 1, 1996): 128–36. https://doi.org/10.1007/BF02686945.

Pariser, Eli. *The Filter Bubble: How the New Personalized Web Is Changing What We Read and How We Think.* London: Penguin Books, 2011.

Perlroth, Nicole, Amie Tsang, and Adam Satariano. "Marriott Hacking Exposes Data of Up to 500 Million Guests." *New York Times,* December 1, 2018. https://www.nytimes.com/2018/11/30/business/marriott-data-breach .html.

Pham, Nga. "Vietnam Admits Deploying Bloggers to Support Government." *BBC News,* January 12, 2013. https://www.bbc.com/news/world-asia -20982985.

Phillips, Whitney. *This Is Why We Can't Have Nice Things: Mapping the Relationship between Online Trolling and Mainstream Culture.* Cambridge, MA: MIT Press, 2015.

Porup, J. M. "How Mexican Twitter Bots Shut Down Dissent." *Motherboard,* August 24, 2015. https://motherboard.vice.com/en_us/article/z4maww /how-mexican-twitter-bots-shut-down-dissent.

Qtiesh, Anas. "Spam Bots Flooding Twitter to Drown Info about #Syria Protests." *Global Voices Advocacy* (blog), April 18, 2011. https://advox.global voices.org/2011/04/18/spam-bots-flooding-twitter-to-drown-info -about-syria-protests/.

Quattrociocchi, Walter, Antonio Scala, and Cass R. Sunstein. "Echo Chambers on Facebook." SSRN Scholarly Paper. Rochester, NY: Social Science Research Network, June 13, 2016. https://papers.ssrn.com/abstract=2795110.

Rankin, Jennifer. "Catalan Independence: EU Experts Detect Rise in Pro-Kremlin False Claims." *Guardian,* November 13, 2017. http://www.the guardian.com/world/2017/nov/13/catalan-independence-eu-experts -detect-rise-in-pro-kremlin-false-claims.

Rasmussen, Tom. "There Was a Tinder Election Bot Fanning the Fire of the Youth Vote." *I-D* (blog), June 15, 2017. https://i-d.vice.com/en_uk/article /3kd87w/general-election-tinder-bot-youth-vote.

Reporters Without Borders. "Vietnam's 'Cyber-Troop' Announcement Fuels Concern about Troll Armies." *RSF,* January 12, 2018. https://rsf.org/en /news/vietnams-cyber-troop-announcement-fuels-concern-about-troll -armies.

Rueda, Manuel. "2012's Biggest Social Media Blunders in LatAm Politics." *ABC News,* December 26, 2012. https://abcnews.go.com/ABC_Univision /ABC_Univision/2012s-biggest-social-media-blunders-latin-american -politics/story?id=18063022.

Sanovich, Sergey. "Russia: The Origins of Digital Misinformation." In *Computational Propaganda: Political Parties, Politicians, and Political Manipulation on Social Media,* edited by Samuel C. Woolley and Philip N. Howard, 21–40. New York: Oxford University Press, 2018.

Schmidt, Selma. "Estudo mostra que menções a Crivella nas redes sociais caiu em três meses [Study shows that mention of Crivella in social networks fell in three months]." *O Globo,* September 4, 2017. https://oglobo .globo.com/rio/estudo-mostra-que-mencoes-crivella-nas-redes-sociais -caiu-em-tres-meses-21180048.

Schreckinger, Ben. "Inside Trump's 'Cyborg' Twitter Army." *Politico,* March 9, 2016. https://www.politico.com/story/2016/09/donald-trump-twitter -army-228923.

Scott-Railton, John, and Morgan Marquis-Boire. "A Call to Harm: New Malware Attacks Target the Syrian Opposition." *Citizen Lab,* June 21, 2013. https://citizenlab.ca/2013/06/a-call-to-harm/.

Shane, Scott, and Alan Blinder. "Secret Experiment in Alabama Senate Race

Imitated Russian Tactics." *New York Times,* March 4, 2019. https://www
.nytimes.com/2018/12/19/us/alabama-senate-roy-jones-russia.html.

Shane, Scott, and Vindu Goel. "Fake Russian Facebook Accounts Bought
$100,000 in Political Ads." *New York Times,* September 6, 2017. https://
www.nytimes.com/2017/09/06/technology/facebook-russian-political
-ads.html.

Shearer, Elisa. "Social Media Outpaces Print Newspapers in the U.S. as a
News Source." *Pew Research Center* (blog), December 10, 2018. https://
www.pewresearch.org/fact-tank/2018/12/10/social-media-outpaces
-print-newspapers-in-the-u-s-as-a-news-source/.

Sherman, Jake. "Poll: 1-in-4 Voters Believe Trump's Vote-Fraud Claims."
Politico, February 1, 2017. https://www.politico.com/story/2017/02/poll
-donald-trump-voter-fraud-234458.

Shipman, Tim. *All Out War: The Full Story of How Brexit Sank Britain's Political Class.* New York: HarperCollins, 2017.

Silverman, Craig. "This Analysis Shows How Viral Fake Election News Stories Outperformed Real News on Facebook." *BuzzFeed News,* November
16, 2016. https://www.buzzfeednews.com/article/craigsilverman/viral-fake
-election-news-outperformed-real-news-on-facebook.

Shirky, Clay. "The Political Power of Social Media." *Foreign Affairs,* December 20, 2010. https://www.foreignaffairs.com/articles/2010-12-20/political
-power-social-media.

Solon, Olivia. "How Syria's White Helmets Became Victims of an Online
Propaganda Machine." *Guardian,* December 18, 2017. https://www.the
guardian.com/world/2017/dec/18/syria-white-helmets-conspiracy
-theories.

"Space: The Next Startup Frontier." *Economist,* June 7, 2014. https://www
.economist.com/leaders/2014/06/07/space-the-next-startup-frontier.

Spenkuch, Jörg L., and David Toniatti. "Political Advertising and Election
Outcomes." SSRN Scholarly Paper. Rochester, NY: Social Science Research Network, April 1, 2016. https://papers.ssrn.com/abstract=2613987.

Stevenson, Alexandra. "Facebook Admits It Was Used to Incite Violence in
Myanmar." *New York Times,* November 6, 2018. https://www.nytimes
.com/2018/11/06/technology/myanmar-facebook.html.

Stimson, Rebecca. "Letter Dated 19 July 2018 from Facebook to the DCMS
Committee." July 19, 2018. https://www.parliament.uk/documents/com
mons-committees/culture-media-and-sport/Fake_news_evidence/Letter
-from-Rebecca-Stimson-Facebook-to-Chair-re-question-29-19-July
-2018.pdf.

Taylor, Emily, Stacie Walsh, and Samantha Bradshaw. "Industry Responses
to the Malicious Use of Social Media." *NATO StratCom COE,* Novem-

ber 2018. https://www.stratcomcoe.org/industry-responses-malicious-use
-social-media.

Terry, Collins. "Twitter's Huge Bot Problem Is out of the Bag." *CNET,* February 1, 2018. https://www.cnet.com/news/twitter-bot-fake-followers
-problem-out-of-the-bag/.

Timberg, Craig, and Elizabeth Dwoskin. "Twitter Is Sweeping Out Fake Accounts Like Never Before, Putting User Growth at Risk." *Washington Post,* July 6, 2018. https://www.washingtonpost.com/technology/2018/07/06
/twitter-is-sweeping-out-fake-accounts-like-never-before-putting-user
-growth-risk/.

"Trust: The Truth?" Ipsos MORI Thinks. 2019. https://www.ipsos.com/sites
/default/files/ct/publication/documents/2019-09/ipsos-thinks-trust-the
-truth.pdf.

Turkle, Sherry. *Alone Together: Why We Expect More from Technology and Less from Each Other.* 3rd ed. New York: Basic Books, 2017.

"UK Statistics Authority Statement on the Use of Official Statistics on Contributions to the European Union." *UK Statistics Authority* (blog), May 27, 2016. https://www.statisticsauthority.gov.uk/news/uk-statistics-authority
-statement-on-the-use-of-official-statistics-on-contributions-to-the
-european-union/.

Umpierre, Flávia. "Dilma vai à justiça contra os robôs de Aécio [Dilma goes to justice against the robots of Aécio]." *Partido dos Trabalhadores,* October 10, 2014. https://pt.org.br/dilma-vai-a-justica-contra-os-robos-de
-aecio/.

Ungerleider, Neal. "Behind the Mystery of Spam Tweets Clogging Syrian Protesters' Streams." *Fast Company,* April 21, 2011. https://www.fastcompany
.com/1748827/behind-mystery-spam-tweets-clogging-syrian-protesters
-streams.

"US Secretly Created 'Cuban Twitter' to Stir Unrest and Undermine Government." *Guardian,* April 3, 2014. http://www.theguardian.com/world
/2014/apr/03/us-cuban-twitter-zunzuneo-stir-unrest.

US Senate. Select Committee on Intelligence. "Testimony of Sean J. Edgett, Twitter, Inc." November 1, 2017. https://www.intelligence.senate.gov/sites
/default/files/documents/os-sedgett-110117.pdf.

Vaidhyanathan, Siva. *Antisocial Media: How Facebook Disconnects Us and Undermines Democracy.* New York: Oxford University Press, 2018.

"Venezuela Ruling Party Games Twitter for Political Gain." *Voice of America,* August 4, 2015. https://www.voanews.com/americas/venezuela-ruling
-party-games-twitter-political-gain.

We Are Social. "Digital in 2017: South America." January 26, 2017. https://
www.slideshare.net/wearesocialsg/digital-in-2017-south-america.

Weiwei, Ai. "China's Paid Trolls: Meet the 50-Cent Party." *New Statesman,* October 17, 2012. https://www.newstatesman.com/politics/politics/2012 /10/china%E2%80%99s-paid-trolls-meet-50-cent-party.

Wertime, David. "Meet the Chinese Trolls Pumping Out 488 Million Fake Social Media Posts." *Foreign Policy,* May 19, 2016. https://foreignpolicy .com/2016/05/19/meet-the-chinese-internet-trolls-pumping-488-million -posts-harvard-stanford-ucsd-research/.

Westen, Drew. *The Political Brain: The Role of Emotion in Deciding the Fate of the Nation.* Reprint ed. New York: PublicAffairs, 2008.

"WhatsApp Bans Hundreds of Thousands of Accounts in Brazil." *Washington Post,* October 19, 2018. https://www.washingtonpost.com/business /economy/whatsapp-bans-hundreds-of-thousands-of-accounts-in-brazil /2018/10/19/0c1fd1a0-d3cc-11e8-83d6-291fcead2ab1_story.html.

"Who Is Using EGHNA Media Server." *EGHNA Media Server.* http://media .eghna.com/success_stories. Accessed June 16, 2014; URL discontinued.

Wojcik, Stefan, et al. "Bots in the Twittersphere." *Pew Research Center,* April 9, 2018. http://www.pewinternet.org/2018/04/09/bots-in-the-twittersphere/.

Woolley, Samuel C., and Douglas R. Guilbeault. "United States: Manufacturing Consensus Online." In *Computational Propaganda: Political Parties, Politicians, and Political Manipulation on Social Media,* edited by Samuel C. Woolley and Philip N. Howard, 21–40. New York: Oxford University Press, 2018.

Woolley, Samuel C., and Philip N. Howard. *Computational Propaganda: Political Parties, Politicians, and Political Manipulation on Social Media.* New York: Oxford University Press, 2018.

———. "Political Communication, Computational Propaganda, and Autonomous Agents." *International Journal of Communication* 10, Special Issue (2016): 4882–90. https://doi.org/10.1177/146144402321466813.

YouGov, and The Economist. "The Economist/ YouGov Poll," 2016. https:// d25d2506sfb94s.cloudfront.net/cumulus_uploads/document/ljv2ohxmzj /econTabReport.pdf.

Acknowledgments

I have many collaborators, coauthors, and organizations to thank for their support, assistance, and creative energy. For their fieldwork, data analysis, scholarly insight, political values, policy investigation, and research assistance, I am grateful to Dan Arnaudo, Nicole Au, Gillian Bolsover, Samantha Bradshaw, Scott Brennan, Mona Elswah, John Gallacher, Bharath Ganesh, Monika Glowacki, Robert Gorwa, Douglas Guilbeault, Ana Grouverman, Alex Hogan, Monika Kaminska, Bence Kollanyi, Mime Liotsiou, Cindy Ma, Nahema Marchal, Sam Maynard, Nick Monaco, Vidya Narayanan, Lisa-Maria Neudert, Erin Simpson, Samantha Shorey, and Sam Woolley. The Graphika team, particularly John Kelly and Camille Francois, are a pleasure to work with. It can be depressing to work on this topic! Being part of this investigative team has made it all manageable, rewarding, and impactful.

Some of the ideas and evidence presented here have appeared in our academic and policy papers. For short passages that are taken from those reports I provide additional acknowledgments with specific citations at the beginning and end of the passages, and for data, interviews, or fieldwork observations made by the team I provide citation to the researcher doing the fieldwork and the pseudonym of the person interviewed.

I thank Yale University Press for its support of the book, in particular Joe Calamia for helping me find ways to keep the normative agenda and hone the message. I am indebted to the editorial, design, and marketing team of the Press for making the agenda and message polished and presentable.

I am very grateful to the community of the Oxford Internet Institute for providing an incredible home for multidisciplinary research. This kind of research used to involve drawing ideas from several different domains of inquiry. Increasingly, it also means doing the public engagement that all those different disciplines are good at. The computer scientists aren't just part of the analytical team. They must help the researchers who aren't computer scientists build and release computational tools for the extended network of investigators. The policy analysts aren't just good at interpreting the machinations of political leaders and industry PR teams. They must help the researchers who aren't policy analysts host and curate workshops so that government and industry can encounter each other on the neutral turf of Oxford University. The field researchers' role is not simply to do participant observation and interviews among varied organizations in faraway places. They coordinate the transfer of research capacity to the civil society groups and journalists we want to assist. I'm obliged to the Oxford Internet Institute, which has become a spectacular incubator for new research and a powerful platform for high-impact tool building, policy engagement, and capacity transfer activities.

I thank the US Senate Select Committee on Intelligence for sharing data. This book and its conclusions are based in part on the analysis of social media content provided by the

US Senate Select Committee on Intelligence under the auspices of the Committee's Technical Advisory Group, whose members serve to provide substantive technical and expert advice on topics of importance to ongoing Committee activity and oversight. The findings, interpretations, and conclusions presented herein are mine and do not necessarily represent the views of the Senate Select Committee on Intelligence or its Membership. All the data provided by the US Senate was for fake accounts operated by the IRA (Russia's Internet Research Agency), not human subjects, and no user data on real human subjects was used in this part of the analysis.

I gratefully acknowledge the support of the European Research Council for the grant "Computational Propaganda: Investigating the Impact of Algorithms and Bots on Political Discourse in Europe," Proposal 648311, 2015–2020, Philip N. Howard, Principal Investigator, and the grant "Restoring Trust in Social Media Civic Engagement," Proposal 767454, 2017–2018, Philip N. Howard, Principal Investigator. Additional support for this research has been provided by the Adessium Foundation, Ford Foundation, Hewlett Foundation, Microsoft Corporation, Omidyar Foundation, Open Society Foundation, and the Oxford Martin School's "Misinformation, Media and Science" program. Any opinions, findings, and conclusions or recommendations expressed in this material are those of the researchers and do not necessarily reflect the views of the funders or the University of Oxford.

I'm very grateful to the people who were willing to be interviewed. They were offered several kinds of protections. The research was guided by the highest contemporary ethical standards, which were reviewed by an independent ethics auditor. As part of these protections, several people and companies have been given pseudonyms. Overall research activities were approved by the University of Oxford's Research Ethics Committee (CUREC OII C1A15-044), with additional approvals to study the flow of misinformation over social media in the United States (CUREC OII C1A17-054) and the activities of fake and trolling accounts (CUREC OII C1A17-076).

Index